Palm Reading for Beginners

PALM READING
FOR BEGINNERS

A Guide to Discovering
Your Strengths and Decoding
Your Life Path

Kenneth Lagerstrom

ROCKRIDGE
PRESS

First Rockridge Press trade paperback edition 2020

Rockridge Press and the Rockridge Press logo are trademarks or registered trademarks of Callisto Media Inc. and/or its affiliates in the United States and other countries and may not be used without written permission

For general information on our other products and services, please contact our Customer Care Department within the United States at (866) 744-2665, or outside the United States at (510) 253-0500.

Paperback ISBN: 978-1-64611-243-2 | eBook ISBN: 978-1-64611-244-9

Manufactured in the United States of America

Interior and Cover Designer: Antonio Valverde
Art Producer: Janice Ackerman
Editor: Sean Newcott
Production Editor: Jenna Dutton
Production Manager: Giraud Lorber

Custom illustations © Bambi Ramsey

10 9 8 7 6 5 4 3 2 1

To my father,
Robert—my reason,
my inspiration,
my motivation,
my dad.
Requiescat in pace.

CONTENTS

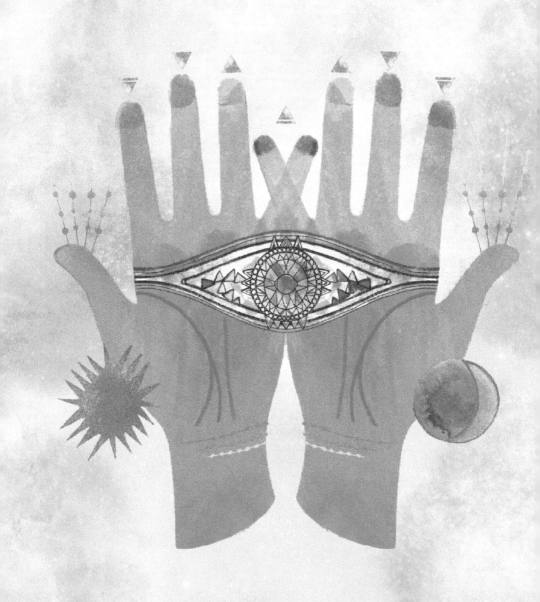

INTRODUCTION

H and analysis, or palmistry, is one of the oldest known fields of study. Continually evolving and developed over millennia, the study of the hands and their markings has captivated the attention of both scholars and initiates since prerecorded history. Clearly, it has captivated your attention as well, which brought you to *Palm Reading for Beginners.*

Writing a book for beginners on the study of the hands was not easy because there is so much detail and so many topics that interact with each other when analyzing just that one part of the body that a complete work on the subject would require an enormous manual. Nevertheless, I have endeavored to present the essential information you need to get started in an easy-to-understand yet comprehensive manner. By the time you finish this book, you will have the knowledge you need to perform a thorough analysis of anyone's hands, especially your own.

When you go to someone to have your palm read, the information they offer has the potential to influence your behavior. Unfortunately, there are many shady palm readers out there, and that is why I got into teaching palmistry. My thoughts were that if I could educate people on the basics, they would have more information than any of those so-called professionals could offer and do a thorough reading for themselves.

Studying the hands has had a huge influence in my life. Through palmistry, I was able to better understand my own motivations and potentials. Of course, I still have some negative habits and emotional responses—palmistry doesn't magically fix those. It did, however, give me a deeper understanding of these traits, allowing me to overcome many personal challenges that could have taken years of therapy to deal with. It's not only my life that has been changed by palmistry. As a professional reader, I have been consulted by many powerful individuals looking to make the best decision possible for their specific circumstances. These readings tended to be the most challenging because my interpretations, consisting of only a few words or sentences, were acted upon, thereby influencing the lives of countless others. I carefully read what I saw and they made their decisions based on that, feeling positive about their choices.

When first starting out, refer to your books and other learning materials as much as you need to. Go back and forth between your hands and these pages. It's a bit of a slower way to learn, and it might seem harder to understand at first, but reading palms is a labor of love that you can and will master if that is what you aim to do. A firm grounding in accurate palm analysis will prove indispensable when putting multiple markings and traits together to understand their interaction and results for yourself as well as others.

It takes a great deal of time to master the skills of a palm reader. Even if it takes you a while to glean just one additional piece of information, it is worth it because that is one more piece of the puzzle you didn't have before. Your skills will improve as you continue to practice and increase your knowledge base. There are a number of ways to approach palmistry, as it is an ancient and enchanting practice, and while this book will provide you with an essential and enlightening understanding of palm reading, I encourage you to remain a curious student of palmistry and continue to expand your understanding.

PART
one

UNDERSTANDING
PALMISTRY

CHAPTER
1

The HISTORY of PALM·READING

Any structure will fail if it doesn't have a solid foundation, and palmistry is no different. Each learning step builds on the one before it, so let us begin creating your foundation by starting with a few basics and then going back to the beginning. With the history and other essential information covered in this chapter, you will gain a sense of how modern palm reading came into being, and how it has evolved into the art and science it is today.

Palm Reading Basics

Unlike other divination practices, such as tarot cards, birth charts, and rune casting, the only reading material you need when reading a palm is the palm itself. Simply put, palmistry is the interpretation of characteristics and markings on the hands (both the dominant and nondominant hand) in an effort to understand a person's past, present, and *possible* future.

Perhaps the biggest misconception about palm reading has been that it predicts *the* future. However, there is no predetermined fate that cannot be altered. I believe that American author and poet Ella Wheeler Wilcox said it best when she wrote:

"There is no chance, no destiny, no fate,

Can circumvent or hinder or control

The firm resolve of a determined soul."

Even if the palm markings on a person's hands show remarkable and imminent successes, the person still must act on them to achieve their promise. A favorable palm reading won't just automatically come true if that person takes a passive approach to life. This is also true for so-called negative signs; these can be overcome or modified with correctly applied efforts.

In addition to avoiding absolutes, there's much to be aware of when learning to read hands. Perhaps the best advice I can give you is to learn from the most knowledgeable instructors you can. Beware of websites with little information and many ads, as these are often not reliable sources of information. Ignore any guidance that says, "This line *always* means this."

If you are seeking to have your palm read as a basis for comparison, steer clear of readers who simply say what their clients want to hear or who use a fear-based analysis. A good example of a shady reading method is known as "cold reading"—a parlor trick or mentalist technique to get a person to reveal information about themselves without realizing it. Competent palm readers will be happy to explain how they reached their interpretations based on what they see in your hand rather than tell you it is a trade secret or only something you can learn in one of their courses. However, if you trust the person reading your palms, there is no reason *not* to answer their questions. The insight you can gain from cooperating with a reputable reader will only benefit you.

Above all else, when getting your palms read, remember to never fall for the "you've had a curse put on you, but I can remove it" swindle. Yes, people still fall for this scam, as they did in the old days when palm reading was done in secret. Those who promise they can provide curse removal, new love, or wealth should be handled one way: run away from them. This is not palmistry in any way, shape, or form.

Finally, when studying palmistry, be aware of what is known as the Forer effect (also called the Barnum effect). This phenomenon is based on a 1948 study by Bertram R. Forer, in which he gave multiple people the same general personality analysis. Forer's experiments showed that a majority of people would believe that the general information accurately and specifically applied to them. This study is often used in error by skeptics as "proof" that palmistry does not work. A proper reading prioritizes markings by their importance for that individual hand, making it much more accurate and personalized. If you choose to replicate this study with palmistry, have the person's close associates evaluate the reading for accuracy, rather than the person themselves. Many traits shown on the palms can be difficult to accept, especially if they are challenging areas that could be improved. Even if you are not performing a study, an outside perspective can be helpful.

Palmistry Through the Ages

The origins of palmistry (used here generically to mean any and all aspects of cheirology, the study of the hands) predate written history. Like astrology, which is perhaps the only divination method as ancient as palm reading, the art of interpreting the hands was already well developed before we had written language. Other divination practices such as tarot, runes, and the I Ching (a manual of divination based on symbolic trigrams and hexagrams) came about only after written languages were created. Incidentally, some hand-reading practitioners hold that Norse runes were fashioned after markings found on the palms. In fact, with little exception, the rune meanings actually parallel the common interpretations of the same palmistry markings. Let's now take a short tour through the history of palmistry.

FROM MYTHS AND LEGENDS TO WRITTEN ACCOUNTS

Ancient Greek mythology held that palmistry originated with the creation of man. It was considered to be a gift from Hermes, god of prophesy, intuition, and inspiration. The Bible also dates it back to the creation of man, with a passage that reads, "And God placed seals (signs) on the hands of man so that all men may know their works" (Job 37:7). Other claims as to the origins of palmistry credit its creation to the Chaldean magi of pre-Babylonian times and the priests of Isis in Egypt.

Moving forward from myths and legends, the earliest written accounts of palmistry originated with the Brahmins (Hindu priests) in India thousands of years ago. In the ancient Purusha Sukta of the Vedas (Hindu scriptures), it is said that the Joshi caste (Brahmins) were the teachers and instructors of hand reading. As Hinduism spread outside of India, it brought along an understanding of hand analysis. As a result, China, Tibet, Egypt, and Persia all began to develop their own systems. (Interestingly, North American native tribes also developed systems of palmistry, but seemingly independent of these other methods.)

In China, palmistry was widely used as far back as the Zhou dynasty (1046–256 BCE). During the Western Han dynasty (206 BCE–24 CE), China developed a new system of palmistry with a focus on health and luck, which differed greatly from those of the Indian and Western styles. Early Taoist Chinese palmistry looked for "trigram" (three-line) patterns on the palms, considered to be as important as the major lines. These would then be interpreted according to the I Ching to determine if a person's path was favorable or unfavorable. Another notable difference is interpreting the "single transverse palmar crease" (also known as the Simian Line, discussed in chapter 5). In Chinese palmistry, it is still considered a "good" mark for men, but a "bad" mark for women.

THE DEVELOPMENT OF MODERN WESTERN PALMISTRY

Ancient Greece is considered the birthplace of modern Western palmistry. The markings on the hand were renamed and interpretations modified according to Greek philosophy and religious views. The modern word *cheirology* literally means "hand science," and the Greeks embraced it as one of their fields of higher study. Anaxagoras (c. 423 BCE) is one of the earliest historical palmistry practitioners and teachers, but Aristotle himself is probably the most notable figure who studied and developed the art.

The Roman Empire also embraced palmistry, modifying the system to incorporate Roman religious beliefs and adapt the Greek analysis methods to use Latin names. In fact, many of the modern English terms we use in hand analysis today are taken from the Latin.

A Forbidden Art

During the Middle Ages, the Catholic Church enforced that only through God could one know one's path. Any other method of gleaning information was condemned, punishable by death. All methods of divination, including cheiromancy (palmistry), were forbidden. Satan was believed to be the "father of palmistry." As a result of the fear this invoked, much of the knowledge in Western hand-reading methods was lost.

Even today, there are some religions that prohibit palmistry. To those who may rely on religious texts and teachings for their beliefs on palmistry, I would remind them that the basis for religious prohibition is on predicting *the* future. Observing natural patterns and their logical outcomes is in no way decried or denied. If you see yourself driving toward a deep cliff, it would be foolish to keep going straight. In the same way, palmistry can show only the natural progressions and logical outcomes, not the certain or preordained future. Using palmistry to predict *the* future may be emphatically prohibited, but using any method you can to improve your own life and your contribution to the lives of others has been and still is encouraged.

Note also that some religions such as Hindu and Buddhism suffered no such lengthy and widespread suppression of divination and, in fact, officially promoted or endorsed it.

Along with other methods of divination, palm reading fell into disrepute during the Middle Ages (see "A Forbidden Art" on page 8). After being banned by the Catholic Church, the practice was picked up by vagabonds, who often had only rudimentary knowledge of the art and could be quite unscrupulous in their goal of removing coin from their querents. Fortunately, there were a few who retained and taught the deeper meanings and secrets of the art, which we know today. It wasn't until the early 1900s that palmistry began to experience a renaissance in the West.

Palm Reading Today

Modern palmistry starts near the turn of the 20th century when the Cheirological Society of Great Britain was founded in 1889. One of their goals was to eliminate or expose fraudulent palmistry, which would allow for serious focus on the art and science of palm reading. A decade later, hand readers such as Cheiro (the nickname of William John Warner) and William G. Benham took their own extensive studies and published what became foundational books for any student interested in palmistry: *The Benham Book of Palmistry* and *Cheiro's Language of the Hand*. While numerous books were later published, none were considered the invaluable references that Cheiro's and Benham's books were.

With newer and more accurate information readily available to the general public, the interest in scientific palmistry increased. With book in hand, there was no longer the need to travel extensively to study from experts. Then, with the introduction of the Internet, palmistry took another giant leap forward. Experts from around the world were now able to collaborate and share their knowledge and individual styles with one another. This allowed comprehensive works to be developed, such as *The Encyclopedia of Palmistry* by Ed Campbell, which provides even more detail than Benham's book. Published in 1995, Moshe Zwang's book *Palmtherapy* introduced specific techniques of palmar massage to correct or improve psychological conditions, and Arnold Holtzman was the first to establish and clinically prove some psychological analyses through palmistry, discussed in his textbook, *Biometric Definitions of Personality.*

It is the accessibility and availability of information that makes research like this possible. However, the Internet also has its downsides. In our modern world of social media, there is a plethora of misinformation on numerous topics, including palmistry. This can, unfortunately, result in a potential student disbelieving the entire field of study and others concluding that palm reading is a sham or a con intended to take advantage of the weak-minded or gullible. Yes, there are scammers out there, but palmistry is a true art and science. I began as a skeptic, asked the right questions, studied reputable sources, and concluded the accuracy for myself. I suggest you do the same.

How Often Should I Get My Palms Read?

This is a question my clients often ask. When it comes to having your palms read by someone else, my answer is always the same: once is enough unless you have noticed changes in your palm that you cannot interpret yourself. (Contrary to popular belief, the features of the palms can change some-what over time. You can chart these changes on your hands by taking high-resolution photos every six months or so.)

Even though different readers may have different insights, the fundamentals of what any qualified reader can tell you will be nearly the same. However, read your own hands every chance you get—first alongside your books, and then using the printed text only to look up the meanings of markings you hadn't noticed or understood before. With time and practice, you will continually improve the quantity and accuracy of the information you can interpret.

CHAPTER

2

The PURPOSE
of PALMISTRY

C ontemporary palmistry goes far beyond the traditional definition of reading the lines on the palm to predict the future. It also encompasses several other fields of study related to gaining insight from the hands and methods of improving mental clarity and easing the challenges in life. From the basic shape of a person's hands to interpreting fingerprints, these additional fields of study can provide a more detailed and specific analysis than would be possible from looking only at the lines. As with traditional palmistry, anyone's hands from anywhere in the world can be read using the same foundational methods. You need not be limited to a single system of analysis. The four branches of palmistry discussed in this chapter can be combined with minimal contradiction.

The Laws of Palmistry

Our written and spoken languages may be quite different around the world, but our hands all share a single universal language. Various systems of palmistry do interpret markings differently, but this is due to differences in cultural norms. Whether we call it the Line of Fate or Line of Career, it is still the same line. Markings have multiple meanings depending on our perspective, but they can still provide an accurate and illuminating reading.

The Simian Line, which is a combination of otherwise two distinct lines, is an example of how cultural norms can have an effect on a reading. In Chinese palmistry, a Simian Line is considered lucky for men but unlucky for women. Meanwhile, in Native American palmistry, the Simian Line is considered a positive, powerful sign on any hand, regardless of gender. It is the same mark, but when men and women have vastly different roles in their culture, the interpretations are different. Both interpretations are correct because each is based on the cultural and social expectations of where the person with the Simian Line lives. In other words, a sign may be called one of "luck" or "divine influence," but it really just comes down to perspective.

Another common similarity among most of the different systems is the understanding of how the conscious mind and the subconscious mind interact in the hands. You can think of the conscious mind and the subconscious mind as energies moving between the wrist and the fingertips. The conscious mind starts at the fingertips where it is strongest and moves down to the wrist, becoming weaker. The subconscious moves from the wrist where it is strongest to the fingertips, growing weaker the farther it goes. So the lower part of the palms is primarily subconscious influence, while the fingertips are the conscious choices. The middle of the hand holds a balance between the two.

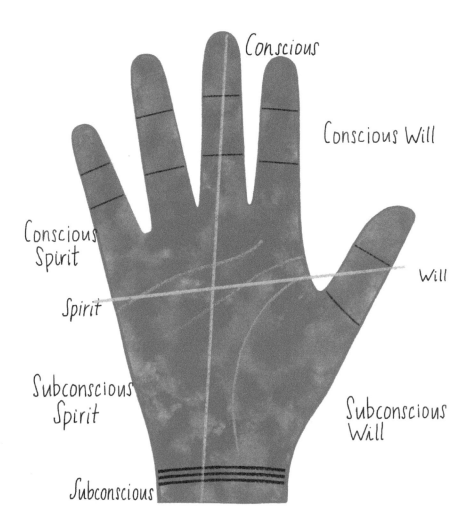

Conscious

Conscious Will

Conscious
Spirit

Spirit

Will

Subconscious
Spirit

Subconscious
Will

Subconscious

Similarly, the willpower and spirit (internal power) start at oppo-site sides and meet in the middle. The will is strongest at the thumb, while the spirit begins on the little finger side of the hand. By looking at these energy movements through the hands, you can see that they create four distinct quadrants: conscious spirit, conscious will, sub-conscious spirit, and subconscious will. When reading hands, keep these quadrants in mind.

The Branches of Palmistry

There are four main branches of palmistry that must be considered to do a comprehensive analysis: cheiromancy, cheirognomy, dermatoglyphics, and cheirokinesics. In part 2, I cover the basics of the first two branches, cheiromancy and cheirognomy, but I want you to be familiar with the other two as well, so I will briefly discuss them in this section and provide you with some foundational knowledge that you should incorporate into your readings.

Any one of these four branches can be used independently of the others and still provide a good degree of accuracy. However, when all four branches are combined, it is like having all the pieces of a jigsaw puzzle. You can still glean what the picture might be with only a quarter of the pieces, but you may also wind up misinterpreting the bigger picture. Like all aspects of cheirology, any one of these four main branches could take a lifetime to master. Study and practice are the only ways to gain proficiency.

CHEIROMANCY

Cheiromancy is the divination and prediction part of hand analysis. For most people, the words *cheiromancy* and *palmistry* are interchangeable. This branch looks primarily at the lines of the palms and fingers, and is probably the most ancient of the four main branches.

There are five major lines examined in palmistry as well as minor lines (these are discussed in chapters 6 and 7). Each line indicates a different part of the self. Cheiromancy examines the lines for traits such as length, color, broken or unbroken appearance, and where on the hand it starts and terminates. Minor lines and individual markings like the Cross or Circle are also looked for and interpreted. Cheiromancy will be covered more in part 2.

CHEIROGNOMY

Cheirognomy is the study of the shape and structure of the hands. This includes hand size, shape, and flexibility, as well as the fingernails, individual finger lengths, and the areas of the palm that are elevated or depressed (known as the mounts of the palm). Cheirognomy is not a divination practice, but rather it shows many of the personality traits, strengths, and weaknesses. The shape of the fingers is a very important part of this field of study. The basic hand shape will provide basic interpretations, while the bends in the fingers and shapes of the fingertips give more in-depth details. Cheirognomy will be covered more in part 2.

DERMATOGLYPHICS

Dermatoglyphics literally translates to "skin carvings." These are the fingerprints and the similar patterns found across the entire palm. This can be the most scientific branch of hand analysis, because these patterns never change during a person's lifetime. The unique patterns of dermatoglyphics are genetic; they appear as early as the fourth month of pregnancy. As with every other sign on the hands, each fingerprint shows but one trait. It is the combinations of prints along with the rest of the dermatoglyphic patterns that reveal a more complete picture.

The location in one of the four quadrants of any dermatoglyphic pattern on the hands helps determine how it is interpreted. (Refer back to the illustration on page 15.) Each fingerprint has its own pattern, which means these are all primarily related to the conscious mind for analysis. Patterns found at the base of the hand are far more related to the subconscious. Be sure to always interpret dermato-glyphic patterns according to the part of the hand on which they are found.

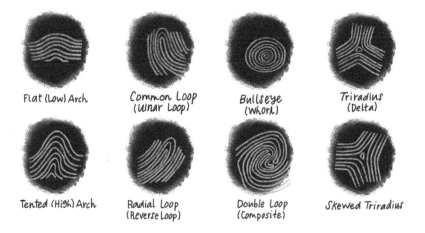

Flat (Low) Arch   Common Loop (Ulnar Loop)   Bullseye (Whorl)   Triradius (Delta)

Tented (High) Arch   Radial Loop (Reverse Loop)   Double Loop (Composite)   Skewed Triradius

The main dermatoglyphic patterns you will encounter are the arch, loop, whorl, and triradius. Each of these also have obvious variations in their appearance. The arch can be low (flat) or high (tented). Loops can be common (ulnar) or reversed (radial). Whorls can be bull's-eyes or composite ("double loop"). Triradii ("delta") can be clear or skewed.

CHEIROKINESICS

Cheirokinesics is the study of hand movements, positions, and gestures. (Kinesics, by the way, is the study of body language in general.) Of all the major branches, cheirokinesics is the most changeable, quickly switching from one interpretation to another. The hands and fingers move almost as quickly as one's thoughts and emotions.

Once you recognize some common hand movements, you will gain an additional understanding of other people's minds, as well as your own. Start by observing your own hand movements and positions both when you are alone and when you are interacting with others. Also observe the same in other people. You will quickly notice how hand movements change much more frequently when

The Meanings of Dermatoglyphic Patterns

FLAT (LOW) ARCH: Denotes traditional values and high morals in adulthood, usually learned through some hardship earlier in life.

TENTED (HIGH) ARCH: Same as the arched pattern but with a higher degree of intellect than the low arch.

COMMON LOOP (ULNAR LOOP): These enter from the little finger side of the hand, lean toward the thumb, then turn back and exit from the same side. They show an ability to draw on ideas from many sources without making anything in particular a focal point in life.

RADIAL LOOP (REVERSE LOOP): These are opposite in appearance to the common loop, entering and exiting from the thumb side. Radial loops are sometimes called the "inventor's mark" and denote a strong ability for innovation and creativity.

BULL'S-EYE (WHORL): These patterns show concentration and intensity, making the area on which they appear a focal point in life. Composite markings denote areas of focus that are controlled equally by the conscious and subconscious.

THE TRIRADIUS (DELTA): This shows where and how three different energies come together and interact. A well-formed pattern indicates harmony and balance. When skewed and not forming equal angles, it denotes an area of conflict or confusion with the larger side being the dominant. Triradii are also used to identify the type of fingerprint in cases where it seems to be a blend of two different types.

we are trying to convey a difficult topic. This is because our brain activity is controlling our movements. Even when speaking on the telephone, it is normal for your hands and fingers to gesture often even though no one can see you.

Hand positions can be chosen and/or used consciously to help draw out and maintain specific thoughts and emotions. The mind controls the hands, but the hands can also lead the mind. Therefore, maintaining specific hand positions and using specific gestures can be an effective method to control your mind or lead your thoughts. Most people in positions of power use calculated movements when interacting with others. With a rudimentary knowledge of cheirokinesics, it is rather easy to understand some of the underlying or hidden messages. Televised political debates are an excellent source to observe and study. Turn off the volume to better focus on the politicians' hand gestures and movements.

To understand the complexity of cheirokinesics, here is an easy exercise to try: For an entire day, keep your hands as still and relaxed as possible. By day's end, you may be shocked at just how often your hands change their resting positions and the number of gestures you use when speaking to others. This is why cheirokinesics is considered one of the most difficult aspects of hand reading to master and why many professionals stick to just the basics when doing readings.

While there are far too many specific hand positions, movements, and gestures to cover in this section, there are a few that are easily recognizable in daily life. Here are a few to be aware of:

+ Hands folded and fingers interlaced is commonly viewed by the average person as a posture of calm refinement; however, these positions usually indicate that constant mental effort is needed to maintain that sense of serenity.

+ The tip of the thumb held against another fingertip(s) shows a conscious effort to control specific energies. These hand positions are commonly found in meditation practices and work to isolate one or more parts of the self for contemplation and awareness.

* Fingers may be observed as contracted, neutral, or extended. A contracted finger denotes that the energies are being focused inward, rather than projecting or interacting with others as with the extended fingers. Neutral (relaxed) shows an area that is passive and neither internalized nor projected outward.

With regard to the fingers themselves, each finger represents different aspects of the individual. Sometimes they are referred to as ego or physical for the index finger, superego or mental for the middle finger, id or emotional for the ring finger, and libido or spiritual for the little finger. Any single aspect projected on its own is weak (such as when a person is just displaying their ego with an extended index finger). When more than one finger moves the same way (extending or contracting), they work together to amplify each other's traits.

The Journey to Self-Discovery

As you read this book and learn to analyze your own hands, you will gain a deeper understanding into your own life path and your connection to the world around you. Learning to read your own hands can be extremely satisfying and empowering. What's more, you'll always have reading material no matter where you are in the world!

I encourage you to begin studying palmistry with a skeptical attitude and allow yourself to arrive at your own conclusions by practicing what you are learning, and there is no better way to practice than on yourself. The art of palm reading is a path of self-awareness and discovery. It can reveal your strengths, weaknesses, and areas where you may be causing unnecessary difficulties in your life. With this knowledge, you can figure out which way to go to bring about the best outcomes.

This isn't guesswork, and you are not expected to be clairvoyant. You will be working with the information that is presented to you in the lines and features of your hands. Intuitive and clairvoyant methods of hand reading are separate arts. A reader may use physical contact with the hands to glean information, but a true reading utilizes the interpretation of the specific and recognizable patterns, which you are learning in this book.

When you feel comfortable doing a reading, you can assist others as well by reading their hands. If you are a parent, being able to read hands can also help you understand your child's unique path and characteristics. But whatever your goals may be, reading your own hands is an internal journey to self-discovery.

What is it that makes you unique and sets you apart from everyone else in the world? From the shape and structure of your hands, you find your primal motivations and character. The lines themselves show the way you think and feel, and how you act on those thoughts and feelings. Your fingerprints show the parts of yourself that cannot be changed but must be adapted to. We might not always like what we see on our palms or in ourselves, but awareness of these characteristics is what allows us to change and improve those parts of ourselves we might consider to be less than optimum.

PART
two

HOW TO
READ PALMS

CHAPTER
3

The FOUR-ELEMENT SYSTEM

As you've learned, cheirognomy is the study of
the shape and structure of the hands. This field
was introduced in the 19th century by French
army officer Captain D'Arpentigney, as noted in *The
Benham Book of Palmistry*. D'Arpentigney was not trained
in palmistry; rather, he gained his knowledge by examining thousands of hands with the intent to eliminate any
predictive elements of palmistry and develop a more scientific approach that would better reflect an individual's
character and inclinations.

Although cheirognomy was intended to be a completely separate field from cheiromancy, it was quickly
embraced by palm readers and incorporated into their art.
In this chapter, you will learn how to identify the basic
hand types you may encounter in a palm reading and the
personality traits they represent. This will provide you
with additional information on which to formulate the
takeaways of your analysis.

Identifying Hand Types

The first step in cheirognomy is to identify the hand type. There is a method that distinguishes seven different shapes, but the Four-Element system is a widely recognized and accepted method of identifying the main hand types and will serve you well in your journey to palm reading.

First, look at the palm itself. It can be viewed as either square-shaped or rectangular. It doesn't have to form a perfect square or rectangle—just gauge a basic comparison of length to width. When notably longer from wrist to the base of the fingers than from side to side across the palm, the palm is considered rectangular. When the length to width is roughly equal, the palm is considered square. A square palm denotes emotional stability and balance, whereas a rectangular palm denotes a degree of instability and insecurity.

Next, look to the length of the fingers. When smaller by comparison to the length of the palm, they are considered short. When almost equal or larger in length compared to the palm, they are considered long. Short fingers show quick judgment and impulsiveness, while long fingers tell of the ability to see the abstract and express oneself intellectually. Long fingers are typically more slender than short ones, with the knuckles more pronounced.

These square/rectangular and short/long observations provide four possible combinations for hand types as follows:

* **Earth hand**—Square palm with short fingers

* **Air hand**—Square Palm with long fingers

* **Fire hand**—Rectangle palm with short fingers

* **Water hand**—Rectangle Palm with long fingers

EARTH

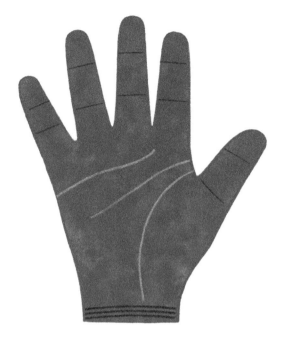

The earth hand combines the stability and practicality of the square palm with the impulsiveness of short fingers. As with all four hand types, these traits have strengths and weaknesses.

Earth hands tend to be quite realistic and practical. They are often traditional in their views, following the morals and ethics in which they were raised. Earth hands are also practical in character and hard-working in their career. With a strong desire to immerse themselves in nature, you can find them camping or gardening and enjoying their love of the outdoors. This type of hand is loyal and dependable.

Even though earth hands have good emotional control, their emotions tend to run high. In love, they love deeply. In anger, their ire is potent. Physical and athletic activities can help keep their strong emotions under control.

Earth hands tend to have a quick temper and a lack of patience with others. They can be possessive and smothering in their emotional relationships and stubborn in their beliefs. Quick to judge, they will hold on to their anger for a very long time if they feel they have been slighted. Because they can be suspicious of others' motives, they can find themselves in relationship problems of their own making.

AIR

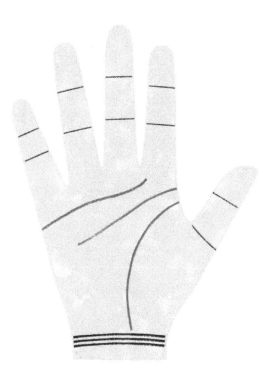

Air hands have the practicality and emotional stability of the square palms, with the intellectual abilities and desires of the long fingers.

Air hands are curious and have a real love of knowledge. They are analytical and look to find order in all things and enjoy organizing their environment. This hand type has natural intuitive abilities and is drawn to the psychic arts. They are extroverted and love to communicate, and will talk your ear off if given the chance.

Air hands are restless and easily bored. They are mistrustful of their emotions and possess an unstable temperament. They can be viewed by others as a walking contradiction. At worst, they can be shallow or superficial and lacking in depth. When slighted, their natural response is to be abrasive and caustic. They are often closed off to ideas or beliefs that are not their own if they cannot be proven.

FIRE

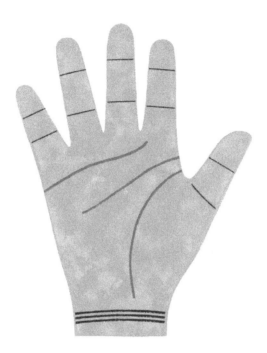

Fire hands have the emotional insecurity of the rectangular palm and the impulsiveness of the short fingers.

With their energy and enthusiasm, they are known for being extremely extroverted, fun to be around, and the life of the party. They are enthusiastic and decisive, basing their quick decisions on intuition. Fire hands love to be active, are very persuasive, and will usually take the initiative in group settings. They love to be on the go and thrive on activity, not realizing that their normal pace can cause exhaustion and burnout. They usually have a positive outlook on life, even during difficult times. This hand type aspires to perfection.

For all their enthusiasm, fire hands have a tendency toward apathy and egocentric thoughts and behavior. Their emotions can change in an instant, from warm and outgoing to cold and aloof. Because fire hands tend to make snap decisions based on intuition, they do not usually think before they act and are often impulsive in their thoughts and actions. They can be very impatient, and speak their mind without tact or forethought.

Preferring to be the center of attention, they can demonstrate great showmanship.

WATER

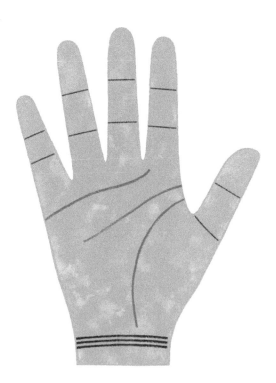

Water hands have the emotional instability of the rectangular palm and the intellect of long fingers.

Water hands are idealists. They are highly creative, sensitive, and intuitive. They tend to be very romantic, immersing themselves in the deep emotions of a relationship. They are sensitive to their environment and can use that sensitivity to enhance their creativity and natural talent in the arts. They are imaginative and solitary, tending to be introverts. When given direction, they show a high degree of confidence.

The strong emotions of water hands can be their downfall. They have difficulty coping with stress and will function best in a calm environment. This hand type has a hard time maintaining mental focus and making tough choices. They can allow their emotions to dictate and run their lives, which can bring out more of their weaknesses than their strengths.

Cautious Cheirognomy

Cheirognomy tends to be very fixed in its interpretations. For example, square hands are seen to indicate emotional stability, while rectangular hands denote lack of emotional control. Although these interpretations can be accurate to a degree, they should not be taken as certainties. Other characteristics will influence a reading and must be factored in for accuracy in the analysis. By also reading the lines of the palm, which you will learn to do in upcoming chapters, and combining those interpretations with cheirognomy, you can find conflicting information that brings light to a bigger picture.

Here is an example: You might find a rectangular hand with a clear and deep Line of Heart on the palm. The hand shape tells of insecurities, while the Line of Heart shows emotional balance and serenity. Both traits must be considered, as they are both natural predispositions. Together, they could indicate a great deal of practice in activities that stabilize the emotions, such as meditation or yoga.

Conflicting traits do not cancel each other out but rather blend to create a combination of both.

Cheirognomy and cheiromancy work hand in hand: no single trait or marking can be interpreted on its own. We are complicated beings with a multitude of motivations and habits. A person who dislikes their job could be the most reliable employee. Someone with promiscuous desires could be a loyal partner for life. The more information you can glean in a reading, the clearer and more accurate the analysis will be.

After you have gained a degree of proficiency in these two fields, I recommend adding dermatoglyphics into the mix (see page 17). This will add to the number of contradictions you discover, but they will help reveal a more complete picture of the person and their unique nature.

Exploring Compatibility Through Readings

It is possible to assess whether or not two people will get along based on their hands. People who have similar palm shapes and finger lengths tend to be compatible. When either the palm shapes or finger lengths are similar, there is still a moderate degree of compatibility. However, when both the palm shape and finger length are different, the pair is far less compatible than average, so they often won't see eye to eye.

In this vein, two people who have the same hand-type combination—air hand and air hand, for example—will be the most compatible. The two typically incompatible element combinations are earth hand/water hand and air hand/fire hand. This must still be factored in with other signs and markings of the hands. Also keep in mind that this is only the basis for a compatibility analysis and cannot be considered a rigid constant. The old quote still applies—sometimes "opposites attract."

CHAPTER

4

OBSERVING
the HAND

T ake your time to fully examine the hands before beginning your analysis. Each marking, sign, or characteristic reveals another piece of the whole picture. What might seem like a minor anomaly can, in fact, have a profound impact on the overall interpretation. The interaction of influences, whether the same traits or opposite, is what paints the complete picture and makes each hand unique. With practice, you will learn to understand each marking and trait, regardless of whether it is a common sign or a one-of-a-kind appearance.

Hand Variations

When examining the hands, it is important to look for features that stand out as different from the average. Any distinguishing characteristics will point to unique aspects of one's personality. Traits to be considered are the basic hand size, individual finger lengths, fingertips and nails, flexibility, and skin texture. Each provides additional insight into a person's character and motivations. I do not include commentary on average-size hands and fingers, as these are a blend between the long and short or wide and narrow, and in this case this information will have little significance to the reading.

HAND SIZE

Hands can be viewed as large, medium, or small. You can't just measure the length with a ruler; you determine this trait by considering the hand size in relation to the person's height. Tall people naturally have larger hands, but the hands could still be considered small. Likewise, a short person could have large hands even though their hands are smaller than the average person's. Large and small hands are easily identified with a quick glance. Both stand out as visually unusual compared to the rest of the person's body.

People with large hands are suited to fine, detailed work. They can immerse themselves in the tiniest details or a project for hours on end. A good example of this was Earl Owen, a renowned microsurgeon who led the team that performed the world's first hand transplant. Owen had some of the largest hands ever seen and had to get all his surgical gloves special ordered because of his enormous hand size.

Conversely, small hands indicate someone who does not fare well with minor details, but easily sees the "big picture." They are natural organizers and project managers, readily able to delegate tasks and oversee the results. People with small hands are often found active in leading roles in politics or special interest groups.

CONSISTENCY AND FLEXIBILITY

Hands can be classed as hard or soft, and rigid or flexible. These classifications show where the person may have great physical endurance or be hardheaded with firmly fixed ideas.

HARD AND SOFT HANDS

Hard hands will feel almost like rock when you press on them, with little or no give in the muscles. This shows a physically active and robust individual, with seemingly endless energy and endurance. They have a love of the outdoors, whether through extended camping and hiking excursions or endless gardening. These people do not belong behind a desk in their career but rather need constant movement and outlets for their physical strength.

Soft hands are exactly the opposite, ill-suited to occupations that are strenuously physical in nature. The muscles are not overly firm but sink in easily when pressed on. Soft hands may still have a fondness for the outdoors but prefer "glamping" rather than roughing it or living off the land. Soft hands show a much more sensitive personality, one that is typically well-suited to vocations where they can be physically inactive. Soft hands are more inclined to careers that utilize either intellect, emotion, or both.

FLEXIBLE AND RIGID HANDS

The flexibility of the finger joints shows the flexibility of ideas and beliefs. Gently push back the fingers one at a time on each knuckle to see if it will bend backward or seems as if it will break before bending. Flexible hands will have many of the knuckles easily bending backward, especially the tip and the base of the fingers. Flexibility means adaptability in thought, belief, and actions. Some degree of flexibility is optimum, but when the fingers bend too easily and far back, the changeability in one's nature typically leads to a lack of the consistent effort required for completion of goals. Their interests simply change too fast and depend on current circumstances and the people around them.

Rigid hands are those where the knuckles will not bend backward at all, especially at the tips of the fingers. (Flexible fingertips will bend back between 45 to 90 degrees.) This denotes firmly fixed and unchanging views, typically following traditional beliefs and showing an unwillingness to change any of their own behaviors. Hard hands are often found accompanying rigid fingers, making their hardheaded nature even stronger.

FLEXIBILITY OF THE THUMB

One very revealing trait is the flexibility of the thumb. The top knuckle under the fingernail reflects the morals and ethics and the general adaptability to new environments and people.

Those with a rigid knuckle are firmly fixed in their responses to those around them. Their personality does not vary depending on who they are with. They dislike change and prefer familiar environments where they feel comfortable.

A very flexible thumb (also known as the "hitchhiker's thumb") bends back easily to a 90-degree angle. This identifies someone who lives for constant variation and changes to their environment and social circles. Their chameleon-like personality finds them feeling quite at ease after just a few minutes in any new circumstances, basically becoming the same as those they are with at the time. The love of variation is so strong that they will rarely consider if the change is a good one or will lead them down a more negative path. Because of their changeable nature, they easily duplicate and then exceed the strengths of those around them, regardless of any personal ethical concerns. In a group of philanthropists, they will improve more lives. With a group of thieves, they will plan a better heist. Their associates and environment create their personality, so they need to choose friends carefully.

One unusual trait for analysis is when the thumb knuckle is rigid and fixed, but because it is naturally bent back, it appears to be flexible. This shows a need for constancy and consistency in their associates and environment but accompanied with the love of variation and change. In this case, the morals and ethics remain fixed, but their need for constant change forces them to adapt in order to act on new opportunities. They will change only as much as is absolutely required. Other people, however, see only the constantly shifting interests and generally view them as having lower moral standards than they actually possess.

TEXTURE

Hand texture refers to the condition of the skin. With thin skin, the veins are easily visible, and the skin is easily moved with a light touch. The expression "thin skinned" applies as the person will be quite sensitive and easily wounded or hurt. When the skin is thick, we see the opposite: little sensitivity to others and not easily hurt by others' words and actions. Coarse skin shows an abundance of physical energy, but with a less-refined personality overall.

Be aware that as we age, our bodies naturally decrease the thickness of the skin. Producing less collagen and elastin makes the skin thinner, while at the same time the loss of some of the fatty layer under the skin adds to this thin appearance. Interpret this as the wisdom we gain with age. With wisdom, we gain additional sensitivity to our environment and circumstances, which is reflected in the skin itself.

FINGERS

The length of the individual fingers can be examined to interpret many character traits. Just as when looking at the hand as a whole, a short finger shows quick judgment and impulsiveness. A long finger tells of more refinement, a desire for intellectual thoughtfulness, and a need to express themselves.

Individual finger lengths are identified by comparing the length of the fingers to each other, rather than to the hand size. The fingers could be seen as short in comparison to the hand, but a single digit could still be classified as long. In this case, there is still the impulsiveness of the short fingers, but a degree of refinement in a single area when compared to that person's normal character.

The middle finger (also known as the finger of Saturn, the second finger, or the mental finger) is normally the longest one. Since this digit sits in the center of the hand, it acts as a balancing factor in the personality. If it is found to be short, only as long as the index and ring fingers, there is little such balance. This relates to instability and lack of control with little interest in intellectual pursuits.

The normal-length index finger (also called the finger of Jupiter, first finger, or physical finger) reaches to the halfway point of the distal phalanx (fingernail segment) of the middle finger. Reaching higher than this is considered long and shows natural language skills, increased ambition, career focus, confidence, and a desire to lead others. A shorter than normal index finger denotes a lack of ambition and some difficulty in learning new languages.

The normal-length ring finger (also called the finger of Apollo, third finger, or emotional finger), like the index finger, reaches to the halfway point of the distal phalanx (fingernail segment) of the middle finger. Longer than this shows a technical mind with natural skills in science and mathematics. A short ring finger shows increased impulsiveness and difficulty learning and expressing new ideas and concepts, especially in science. If the ring finger extends past the length of the middle finger, it shows an excess of risk-taking behavior. These people will gamble in all things: money, love, and even their own life.

The little finger (also called the finger of Mercury, fourth finger, or spiritual finger) normally reaches just past the top knuckle of the ring finger. Longer than this shows excellent communication skills with others, aptitude for business, and increased desire to understand spiritual matters. A short little finger heightens insecurity and shows difficulty in self-expression.

The thumb usually does not go by any other names in palmistry. Its total length normally reaches past the base of the index finger, halfway up the proximal segment (the finger segment closest to the palm). Longer than this shows natural leadership skills with a desire to command and control others. When the thumb is short, there is a lack of willpower and self-control with little natural leadership ability. There's more information on the thumb in "The Revelatory Power of the Thumb" section on page 47.

FINGERTIPS

The fingertips are separated into four categories according to how wide or narrow they are. These four fingertip types in order of width are spatulate, square, conic, and pointed.

Remember that the conscious energy enters through the fingertips and moves its way to the wrist (see page 14). Think of it as water filling a reservoir: once it reaches its peak, it overflows. In the same way, the fingertips must be completely filled before that energy moves past the hands and through the body. This means that wider fingertips with a larger surface area need to process information more completely before making decisions; snap judgments are to be avoided. Fingertips with a small surface area move the vital energy much more rapidly, resulting in quicker decision-making.

SPATULATE

Spatulate fingertips get their name not from the kitchen utensil but from the small, flat medical tool used for mixing and scraping. Spatulate fingertips are the most practical and pragmatic, with virtually all of their efforts going into activities that further their goals. Possessing abundant physical energy, they are almost always on the move doing the things they love with a contagious enthusiasm. Spatulate fingertips prefer physically active competitive sports in their recreation time because they love to stay in motion, but do not usually seek contact sports.

Spatulate fingers tend to avoid doing things by tried-and-true methods, preferring instead to find their own methods. They make great inventors, but only for things that further their goals or personal love of movement. They are highly original thinkers and innovators.

SQUARE

Square fingertips still have a large surface area but not nearly that of the spatulate. They still enjoy physical activity and movement, but that is not their primary motivation. What they desire is organization and order. In their homes, everything has its own place, and they could find anything even with their eyes closed.

Square fingertips have the need to follow established rules and proven methods. In fact, they will balk and be resentful of any attempt to force them to deviate from established norms. They are polite and follow social etiquette to the letter. They are methodical in everything they do and make some of the best athletes because they love practicing and employing fundamental skills.

CONIC

Conic fingertips show a distinctly rounded shape. They are lovers of beauty, quick of thought, impulsive, and intuitive. They find more value in their own personal views of what is beautiful than in the practical value an object holds.

Conic tips love grace and harmony, and they are rather idealistic. They make poor critics due to their inability to accept harsh realities. They fare best in careers that allow them the opportunity to create or admire beauty and creativity and to work with things that inspire. Conic tips would prefer a picture of a unicorn to that of a natural landscape.

POINTED

Pointed fingertips have the smallest surface area, so vital energy moves quickly through the fingers to the wrist. They live almost completely in their own mental world of imaginative dreams and desires. It is as if they live in a higher plane of existence, finding all the most inspirational and spiritually positive things in life.

Pointed tips do poorly in a harsh or physically demanding environment. They can inspire others with their lofty ideals but do not fare well in the real world without someone to support their day-to-day needs. They influence and inspire others to see the visionary and perfect world they hold in their mind. Pointed fingertips almost always have long fingernails.

FINGERNAILS

Fingernails have two main distinctions: short or long, and broad or narrow. This gives us four basic fingernail types. These descriptions refer to the nailbed itself, not the length of nail that grows beyond the fingertip. Even if the nail is bitten down to the quick, look at what would be the natural nailbed.

Long nails have a fairly calm demeanor. They gravitate toward interests such as poetry and the arts. They tend to be gentle and warm in nature, but without great physical strength or endurance. Preferring to see the best in all things, long nails tend to be undiscriminating and find it difficult to be critical and accept distasteful facts.

Short nails indicate more abundance of physical energy and endurance than longer nails. Short nails are highly critical and can make quick judgments by accepting even distasteful facts. Their temper can be quick, and they tend to be skeptics by nature.

The width of the nails shows the variety of interests and activities. Broad or wide nails have numerous interests, both physical and mental. Narrow nails show fewer things that occupy their time and effort.

When a broad nail is also very short, it shows a critical person who likes to get involved in everything happening around them. In other words, they love to meddle in the lives of others, even when their quick judgments are completely unwanted.

The lunula (moons) on the base of each fingernail show the strength of action of the heart. Like some other characteristics of the hands, the appearance of the lunula can change or disappear. When the moons are not visible or only visible on the thumbs, this shows a weaker heart action that would benefit from regular cardiovascular exercise. When the thumb's moon is exceptionally large, it tells that the physical exercise is normally at too high an intensity to be of any real health benefit. (If you have any questions about your cardiovascular health, always consult a physician.)

Anomalies of the Hand

Injuries such as cuts, burns, scrapes, warts, eczema, scars, or amputations as well as other anomalous markings will often be found on both sides of the hands. A mark has meaning and influence for as long as that mark is present. Scars, for example, are permanent markings that will have influence for the remainder of life, but a cut that will eventually heal over will have influence only until such time as it completely fades.

Interpret anomalous markings the same way you would read other hand characteristics. Vertical marks are achievements or advancements; horizontal marks are challenges to overcome. Remember that the back of the hand shows information that is readily visible to others, no matter how much we try to hide it. The palm side of the hand shows information that is more private and for our own personal interpretations. Anomalies found on the nondominant hand typically reflect relationships with family members and, on the dominant hand, indicate the individual themselves and their shorter-term relationships.

Each mark is interpreted according to the mount or area of the hand on which it is found. For example, a vertical cut on the Mount of Jupiter shows an advancement or forward movement in one's ambitions/career. It is still a cut, though, denoting that it is not what the person would have chosen, but rather a positive change that was imposed on them.

Finger segments are particularly revealing for cuts and injuries. As discussed earlier, the four fingers represent the physical (index finger), mental (middle finger), emotional (ring finger), and spiritual (little finger). The bottom segment shows the instinctive level of interaction, the middle segment shows the stimulus response (how we react to other people and environments), and the top segment shows how we choose to act. On a basic level, the middle segment of the ring finger relates to our emotional reaction to the actions of others. A horizontal cut across this segment tells of difficulty in controlling one's own emotions at the time when the cut occurred.

The center of the back of the hand relates to general information on how we are behaving in all social interactions. A stove burn to the back of the hand tells of a feeling of being mistreated by others ("getting burned"). Once again, it is the thoughts and emotions at the time of the injury that are revealing, not the method that caused the injury.

Wood splinters are best interpreted as "something getting under your skin." Look to the location of the splinter to narrow down or identify the issue. A splinter under the index fingernail, for example, would indicate problems in advancing the career ambitions and an undermining of your authority that you are not able to overcome at the moment. (Fingernails represent the protection and defenses we use for that finger's aspect.)

Warts are also interesting to interpret, because they are viewed as circular markings. In palmistry, they can be called "little expressions of hate." A wart on the apex of the Mount of Saturn would be interpreted as ongoing frustration with academic studies or the futility of optimism. Mount injuries and blisters tend to be less revealing than small cuts on the phalanges. Small cuts can identify current issues (as in this present day) much more clearly than other minor injuries.

I have accurately read everything from an ink transfer caused by holding a shopping bag to a severed finger that was bitten off by a monkey. In the case of the shopping bag ink transfer, it was simply a matter of exhaustion that was interfering with thought and logical reasoning. It was a prominent trait in the moment, but quite temporary. With the case of the severed finger, it happened when the person as a child was forced to accompany the parents on a safari-type excursion they did not want to go on. Their belief at the time was that the parents were dictatorial, and because of this, there would never be any chance to express emotions freely.

Go ahead and ask about the circumstances surrounding the creation of the anomaly. This will provide some insight into what the person's mind-set was when the marking or condition was created.

The Revelatory Power of the Thumb

The thumb is sometimes called the "seat of the personality." Several early systems of hand reading would analyze the thumb exclusively, but this provided a less complete analysis.

The thumb has only two segments, whereas the other fingers all have three. It is because of the opposable structure of the thumb that we are better able to use tools and manipulate our environment. Even though the thumb itself has only two segments, readings of the thumb include the metacarpal found in the Mount of Venus (see page 60). This allows for a basic interpretation of three basic areas in life: will, logic, and emotions.

The tip segment of the thumb shows the willpower and forcefulness. If well-developed, the person has the decisive strength necessary to meet their life's challenges head-on and works to overcome them. When appearing thin and underdeveloped, there is usually insufficient strength of character to maintain the efforts needed to face their challenges. When large and overdeveloped, it denotes an almost dictatorial personality who consistently feels the need to get their own way and keep others "under their thumb."

The middle segment shows the logical thinking. When this segment narrows noticeably in the middle and has several vertical lines running through, it shows a refined logic and intellect. The base segment for reading just the thumb is the Mount of Venus, which shows the emotional motivations and passion for life.

CHAPTER
5

MAPPING *the* PALM

T he next step in understanding palmistry is to be able to see how the hand is divided into different areas, each one having its own meanings and the parts of life they influence. These areas are known as the mounts. Examining and interpreting the mounts provide more detail on the character analysis and motivations. When comparing the mounts of both palms, look to see if one hand has a mount that is elevated while on the other it is flat. The dominant hand shows the person's current motivations, while the nondominant one shows more of their background and latent potentials. Normally, if there is a difference in mount elevations between the hands, the dominant hand mount will be more elevated and firmer. Regardless though, look to the dominant hand mounts to see what is present in the here and now.

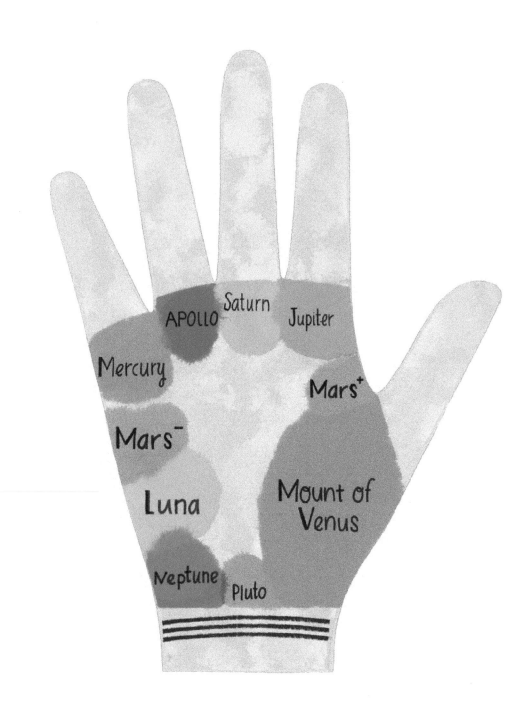

The Mounts of the Hand

The mounts of the hands are the basic zones in which the four types of energy interact. (For a reminder of these energies, see page 14.) Each mount has a separate and distinct way in which it influences the personality. The mounts may be elevated, flat, or depressed. Elevated mounts show a physical and direct approach to the aspect represented by that area. Depressed mounts denote a mental or indirect approach to that aspect. Flat mounts show that the mount in question has no strong influence in the person's life.

When evaluating the mounts, first look to which one is the most elevated and/or strongest (firm, rigid muscle tone). That will show the archetype energy that is most predominant in the person's life. If you are having difficulty assessing which mount is the most elevated, a photocopy or scan of the palm will readily show it by raised areas appearing much darker than the rest of the palm. Note that a mount can be depressed and still be considered strong. The traits represented by the depressed mount are still a dominant factor in life, but those traits are internalized and rarely shared.

JUPITER

The Mount of Jupiter is found under the index finger and governs the physical ambitions. When elevated and firm, it reveals that the person is ruled by their ambition and the desire to command others. Natural occupations for them are in politics, military, and religion, all of which are areas where their desire to command and influence others can be utilized. Because of their endless ambition and willingness to put in the necessary efforts, those with a strong Mount of Jupiter generally attain great success in their chosen field. They are also naturally warmhearted, generous, and extravagant.

Next look to the apex of the mount, seeing if it is highest in the center or leaning toward another part of the hand. With the apex right in the center of the mount, the person will show a good balance between exerting their leadership skills and taking the needs of others into account.

When the peak is found more on the side leaning toward the Mount of Saturn, their ambition and love of command take on a much more serious role. Every leadership decision is thought out in detail before any command is given. Wisdom and sobriety of thought take the forefront. When leaning away from the Mount of Saturn and toward the side of the hand, this denotes the opposite, with primarily selfish and poorly thought-out command decisions.

If the apex is seen leaning toward the Line of Heart (see page 68), their ambitions will be toward their loved ones. Leaning toward the Line of Head (see page 66) indicates the goals are for intellectual and academic endeavors.

If the Mount of Jupiter is depressed, ambitions and leadership potential will be internalized, making their choices safer but bringing about less outward achievement.

SATURN

The Mount of Saturn is located beneath the middle finger. Its realm is the intellectual and serious part of life. The Mount of Saturn is rarely elevated and is frequently seen depressed.

The Saturnian nature is one of seriousness and balance, rarely allowing excitement or enthusiasm to come forth or even be shown. This mount holds the quality of being prudent and somber. They naturally curb the enthusiasm of others, keeping those around them realistic rather than acting on hopes that may prove unfounded or difficult.

A strong Mount of Saturn, whether elevated or depressed, shows a moody personality that does not normally embrace the company of others. They enjoy solitude rather than participation in groups or parties—they are the proverbial "wet blanket." An elevated Mount of Saturn denotes that the person will actively seek to limit the frivolous or exuberant actions of others. When the mount is depressed, they are more thoughtful before they speak but are even more convincing when advising others to tone down their excitement and act more prudently.

APOLLO

The Mount of Apollo appears under the ring finger and shows the expression of the emotions. This mount is rarely dominant on its own; it usually shares its energy with at least one other highly elevated mount.

Apollo aspects are high energy, optimism, enthusiasm, and brilliance. With an elevated Mount of Apollo, there is always the love of beauty, art, drama, and music. They may not be skilled or talented in these arts, but still have a great love and appreciation for them. Even though they are charismatic and have magnetic personalities, they usually do not make long-term friendships because they are simply too changeable in their interests and motivations.

An elevated Mount of Apollo denotes a cheerful and optimistic nature. They may be prone to sudden outbursts of anger, but that is momentary, and they will almost never hold a grudge. This elevated mount also shows a high degree of intuition and rapid learning. Opposite from the Saturn traits of intellectual mastery through study, Apollo denotes quick learning almost through osmosis. Even with a small bit of knowledge on a subject, they will speak of it confidently and will naturally present the appearance of brilliance. Due to their constantly changing interests, they will rarely stay in the same career. They love change, variation, and travel, and will seek vocations that allow for these. Even so, they show the same brilliance and are naturally successful in their endeavors.

The Mount of Apollo can also appear depressed, revealing that all of the traits associated with the elevated mount are internalized rather than expressed easily. (Depressed mounts are usually much firmer in tone than an elevated one.) A depressed Mount of Apollo identifies that although there is a high degree of creativity and love of beauty, the expression is for their own needs and interests, such as a painter who only displays their artwork at home.

MERCURY

The Mount of Mercury is located under the little finger. It governs the areas of commerce and the ways in which we communicate with others. An elevated Mount of Mercury tells of an agile mind, quick judge of character, and shrewdness in business dealings. They make excellent public speakers, physicians, scientists, and lawyers. However, if the rest of the hand shows many negative or weak traits, they may make use of their quick mind and shrewdness to con and take advantage of others. A large inward bending of the little finger reveals a natural temptation toward these negative traits, whether acted upon or not.

A strong Mount of Mercury shows great potential as a businessperson. Few people can outmaneuver them in negotiations or debates, or match them on their intuitive judgment of others' motivations. They are typically excellent in mathematics with few problems they cannot solve.

A depressed Mount of Mercury denotes that they internalize much of their communication ability and scientific ideas, speaking only after careful forethought and calculation.

INNER MARS

The Mount of Inner Mars (also called Mars Positive or Lower Mars) sits above the Mount of Venus and below the Line of Life (see page 71). This is the area of physical courage and martial spirit. When this mount is elevated, it shows a love of physical conflict and rough sports, as well as a natural talent in martial arts.

A depressed Mount of Inner Mars denotes that the person will avoid physical conflict at almost any cost, even if skilled in self-defense. In physical competitions, they prefer noncombative sports.

OUTER MARS

The Mount of Outer Mars (also called Mars Negative or Upper Mars) sits on the little finger side of the hand above the Line of Head (see page 66). It governs mental courage and inner strength. When elevated, it tells of a love of mental competition, whether in debates or games such as chess or poker. This type will resist all efforts to control or limit them more than any other.

A depressed Mount of Outer Mars reveals an active dislike of debates and arguments to the point that they will simply walk away even when they know they are right. Most hands will have one of the Mars mounts elevated and the other depressed.

LUNA

The Mount of Luna is located on the lower part of the little finger side of the hand. This area includes imagination and creativity. This mount is optimally just slightly elevated, not too large and not flat. It is normally only seen depressed when there are underlying health challenges.

A slightly elevated Mount of Luna shows an active and satisfying imagination. These people can experience pleasure from their own mental images and fantasies. This becomes a strong creative force for them, allowing for novel ideas and inventions. However, if the mount is very large, the imagination takes on too much of the mental thoughts and focus. The person is easily distracted or scattered, and mental discipline is too difficult to maintain without a constant practice like meditation.

If the mount is flat, it shows a lack of imagination. Such people find it nearly impossible to create a clear mental image.

VENUS

The Mount of Venus can be found at the base of the thumb inside the Line of Life (see page 71). In this region are the raw passions and love of life. When elevated and smooth, it reveals a sympathetic, generous, warm, and loving personality. Others find them attractive and are naturally drawn to them.

When this mount is flat and the hand flabby, it denotes a person with few or none of these attributes. If the mount is excessively large and the hand flabby, the positive traits shown in the Mount of Venus are lessened by a focus on only romantic love as opposed to universal love.

People with a well-developed Mount of Venus rarely stay single, since so many others are attracted to them.

MOUNT OF NEPTUNE

The Mount of Neptune sits beneath the Mount of Luna at the very base of the little finger side of the hand. This mount can appear elevated or flat, but not depressed. Its realm is the unconscious mind and the depths of self-destructive motivations and behavior. It is also the region of what is termed *telepathy*. Most palmistry systems include this mount as part of the Mount of Luna, but when well-developed and distinctly separate from the Mount of Luna, it denotes a person who is in touch with the interconnected nature of all things. They will frequently know who is calling when the phone rings or who is about to knock on the door.

MOUNT OF PLUTO

The Mount of Pluto lies at the bottom of the palm, centered just above the wrist. It governs basic instincts such as reproduction and survival. This area is almost never elevated, but rather appears moderately depressed. This shows how the individual views life, death, and having children: the deeper the depression, the more they think about and internalize these concepts.

PLAIN OF MARS

The Plain of Mars is the region in the center of the hand, between the Mounts of Inner Mars and Outer Mars. Taking its position in the very center of the palm, this area is of utmost importance in a reading because it is the point of balance where all the mounts interact. Be sure to carefully note the appearance and condition of any lines passing through it. For example, the space between the Lines of Head and Heart (the two largest horizontal markings on the palm) show how we balance thought and emotion in our lives. Any clear markings in this area have a very strong influence in the individual's life choices.

If the Plane of Mars is deeply hollowed with a sunken in appearance, this tells of depression and lack of enthusiasm in all areas of life.

CHAPTER
6

MAJOR PALM LINES

T he lines of the hands, which are often the only thing observed in traditional palmistry, are formed during fetal development by the stimulation of nerves and nerve centers throughout the body but especially the brain. The lines, wherever they appear, show two important details in a person's life. First, each line connects one mount or area to another, allowing the person to blend these attributes. Second, every line also divides or separates one area from another. For every decision made (good or evil, black or white, right or wrong), there will be a corresponding line. These divisions are also the areas in which two opposing forces interact.

It is vitally important to examine the lines on both hands during a reading. Sometimes they will be almost identical in both line placement and mount appearance. In other cases, the palms may look like they are from two completely different people. As a beginner to palmistry, consider the dominant hand to be the "here and now" and the nondominant hand to be the past and latent potential. Changes from the nondominant to the dominant show where efforts have been consistently applied to alter the natural instincts or motivations.

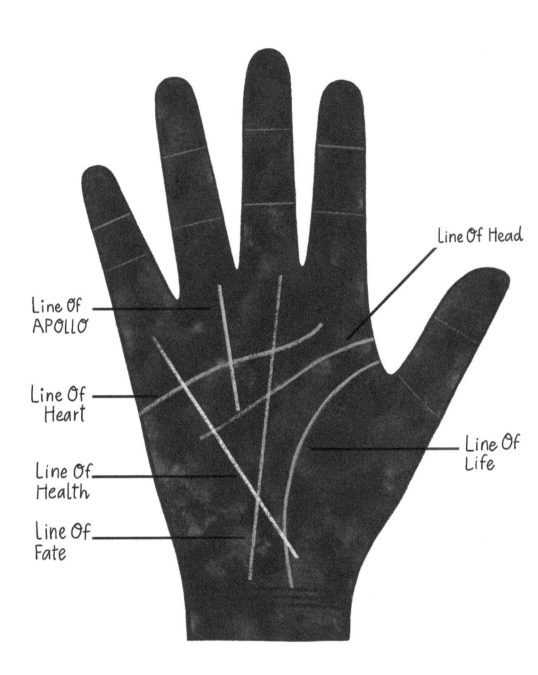

Line Of Head

Line Of
APOLLO

Line Of
Heart

Line Of
Health

Line Of
Fate

Line Of
Life

The Lines of the Hand

There are several major lines of the hand to take into consideration. We will look at each in detail in just a moment, but here is a quick overview:

* The Line of Head (also called Mental Line) shows the basic mentality, cognitive abilities, and deficiencies. Normally running across the center of the hand, this is the basic division and interaction of the conscious and subconscious, or instinct and higher reasoning.

* The Line of Heart shows the strength and condition of the heart and the basis of emotional relationships. It is the division between pleasure and pain.

* The Line of Life is the indicator of the chi energy, or life force, of the individual. It separates life and death, also dividing the passions from the rest of life.

* The Line of Fate (also called Career Line or Saturn Line) shows not only major events but also the belief or denial of predestination and fate. This is the division between spirit and will.

* The Line of Health (also called Hepatica Line or Mercury Line) shows one's general health throughout life. It is the division between sickness and health.

* The Line of Success (also called the Line of Apollo) shows success and achievement from a personal perspective.

LINE OF HEAD

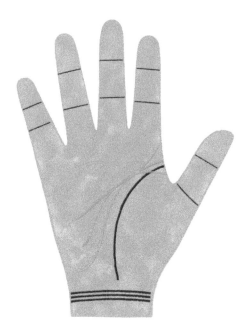

The Line of Head shows a person's basic mentality. It begins near or is connected with the Line of Life just above the thumb, sweeps across the hand, either straight or curved, and usually ends under the ring or little finger. It may appear broad or thin, well defined, or made up of little bits and pieces. The Line of Head may start from inside the Line of Life, above it, or connected to it.

Rising from high on the Mount of Jupiter (see page 55) and widely separated from the Line of Life indicates a highly daring and reckless individual. There is a near total disregard for personal safety and security because they are so confident in their own abilities. The wider the space between the head and life lines, the more this recklessness applies.

When the Lines of Head and Life begin joined together, this shows a sensitive and somewhat insecure individual. When the Line of Head rises, or starts, from inside the Line of Life, it indicates a highly insecure person, inconsistent in thought and action due to doubting their own abilities.

Be sure to note whether the line starts clear and distinct or if it is deeply chained with the Line of Life. The latter is indicative of strong control by parents and the inability to think for oneself for as long as the line remains scattered.

If the Line of Head is found to run straight across the hand to the Mount of Outer Mars, the thinking is focused on the qualities that mount presents: a very practical, business-minded, unimaginative, dogmatic individual. If the Line of Head runs across to the Mount of Luna, the mind takes on the qualities of imagination and creativity.

When found falling sharply to the Mount of Neptune, the mind is strongly influenced by the subconscious. More frequently than average, this indicates a focus on self-destructive thoughts and behaviors. These people often feel an affinity with the "spirit world," and are romantic and idealistic.

When the Line of Head appears clear and deep, it shows practical common sense and the ability to think and act accordingly. Appearing thin and pale, it reflects a colder and crueler nature than that of the clear, deep line. When it is short, barely reaching the center of the hand, this shows a purely materialistic person. Such a person is lacking in imaginative and creative aspects but is right at home in all practical matters.

When chained in appearance or full of little "islands" and hairlines, it tells of headaches, want of concentration, and a lack of fixed ideas.

If the Line of Head should send an offshoot to, or itself turn to another mount, it takes on the qualities of that particular mount:

◆ Toward Luna—Imagination, creativity, mysticism, occult sciences

◆ Toward Mercury—Commerce and science

- Toward Apollo—Desire for fame or notoriety

- Toward Saturn—Music, religion, depth of thought

- Toward Jupiter—Pride, ambition for power

As you can see, each line is affected by where it begins and ends. The beginning shows which area the influence is based on, while the ending shows the direction in which the person is driven by that influence.

LINE OF HEART

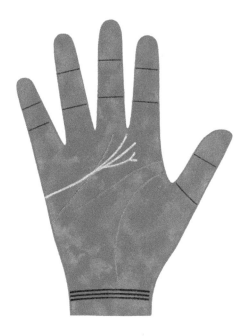

The Line of Heart begins just above the Line of Head on the little finger side of the hand. It can sweep almost straight across the hand or may take a strong upward curve. As with all other lines, you must note its starting point, as this indicates where the line's energy is based.

In some rare cases, the Line of Heart may begin far underneath the Line of Head on the Mount of Outer Mars. This has been referred to as the "Gift of Mercy" and indicates someone who is empathic in nature, keenly feeling the emotions of others. With the line starting so low, however, the entire emotional nature is based on the stubborn and dogmatic qualities of the Mount of Outer Mars.

Where the line travels to is the focus of the heart's energy—where it looks to for the future. Running to the Mount of Saturn, the emotions take on the Saturnian nature: easily offended, serious, and devoted; running to the Mount of Jupiter is just the opposite. These people are ambitious in love and somewhat selfish in nature. They have high ideals for a prospective spouse and will not marry someone they consider "beneath their station," whether this be in money, prestige, or physical appearance. Running between Jupiter and Saturn shows that the focus of the heart is somewhere between these two extremes; the inclination is toward relationships that are not too giving or too taking.

The Line of Heart may also have a forked ending, with one branch going to one area and the other going elsewhere else. This shows that the heart's nature is divided between the two forces, and effort is being exerted on both. As with any other line, if it divides or forks, the total effort is divided between the two, weakening each. If both lines stay strong, it shows that tremendous effort is being exerted to maintain both aspects.

SIMIAN LINE

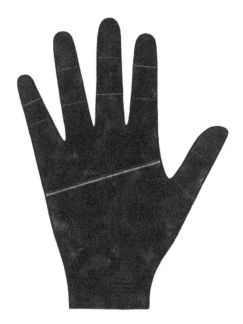

In some cases, the Lines of Heart and Head are not separate at all, but join together to form a single line running straight across the entire palm. This is known as the Simian Line (also called single transverse palmar crease).

When the Simian Line occurs, there is no distinction between what is desired (the heart) and what is thought (the head). The result is an incredible intensity of nature and a strong tendency to rush into things without thinking them through.

With the Simian Line present, there is no Great Quadrangle, which is formed by the Lines of Head, Heart, Health, and Life. The absence of the Great Quadrangle denotes a completely closed-minded individual. Because they are so focused on a particular thought, all else is excluded.

In another possible appearance of the Simian Line, the Lines of Head, Heart, and Life are all joined. All the aforementioned traits apply, but even more intensely since there is no distinction between thoughts, desires, and life itself. These people have the ability to focus on one thing, absolutely, to the exclusion of all else. They generally achieve and accomplish far more than most, developing techniques and inventions that last for generations. They also experience far more heartache and misfortune than most due to this same intensity that drives them. This is truly a double-edged sword.

LINE OF LIFE

The Line of Life rises from the side of the hand above the thumb and grows around the Mount of Venus to the base of the thumb. This line indicates the life force of the individual and separates the passions from the remainder of life. It should be deep, clear, and without any irregularities. Even the smallest variation in this line is indicative of major events in a person's life (something that causes one's life to take a new direction).

When the Line of Life starts low on the hand, this indicates a very introverted person. Notice that the passions (Mount of Venus) do not extend far into the rest of the life. Starting farther up and making a wider circle shows an outgoing nature. The passions extend far out into the other parts of the personality.

Breaks in the Line of Life may take two forms. The first is the overlapping break that indicates a complete change of life. The old way of life "dies" but not before a new way (more extro-verted or introverted) appears. The second form of a break is the clean break. There is no continuation of the life force to the next area. This type of break is usually accompanied by a Line of Mars (see page 81), indicating difficult health issues but a continuation afterward.

An island (see the illustration on page 68) shows a separation of the life force that later rejoins. This indicates a period of weak health or illness.

There is significance to split endings on the Line of Life with one branch running to the base of the Mount of Neptune or if the line leaves its normal position to end beneath this mount. The subconscious passions for experience and satisfaction have pushed the line across the Mount of Pluto, widening the area of impact of the passions in life. The result is a love of change and travel and a deep desire to experience everything life has to offer at least once.

LINE OF FATE

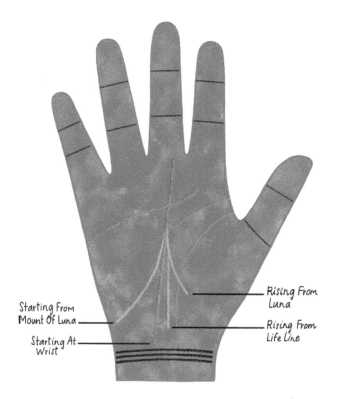

Starting From Mount Of Luna

Starting At Wrist

Rising From Luna

Rising From Life Line

The Line of Fate (also called the Career Line or Line of Saturn) shows the major career aspects and challenges. This line is the major interaction and division of the spirit and will, connecting the subconscious with the conscious choices. At the wrist area, the line shows childhood. Slightly farther up, it shows adolescence and eventually adulthood. When the line reaches the area between the Line of Head and Line of Heart, it reflects ages 35 to 55. Above the Line of Heart is the remainder of the years.

When this line is present (some palms will not have this line or there will be breaks in this line), it means that one's life has a specific direction. When there are breaks in the line, there is no real direction or "higher purpose" to follow during that break.

The Line of Fate may begin from low on the wrist itself or start from as high as the Line of Heart. Any sideways movement is indicative of a change in career or residence. Starting from the wrist itself and running straight up the hand, this placement shows the promise of extreme good fortune in career success. Corroborate this with the Lines of Head and Success.

If the Line of Fate starts low near the wrist and is "tied down" to the Line of Life, this indicates that the person's interests in early life are sacrificed to conform to the wishes and desires of the family. (A "tied down" Line of Fate is one that starts low near the wrist at the middle of the palm, and then as it rises up the hand, it seems to join together with the Line of Life. The Line of Fate then separates again as it continues to rise toward the middle finger.)

If the Line of Fate starts from the Line of Life itself, there is a promise of obtaining success and riches by their own merit. Once again, confirm this with the Lines of Head and Success. As with all other lines, be sure to note its starting and ending points, the clarity and depth of the line, and any modifying markings attached to it. When the Line of Fate rises from the Mount of Luna, the success will depend on the fancy and caprice of others. This is very often the case with celebrities and public favorites.

The higher up it takes for the Line of Fate to appear on the palm, the longer that person's life remains changing and without direction. If the Line of Fate rises from the Line of Head or the Plain of Mars, it indicates that the person will have a hard early life and the successes that are achieved will be hard won.

The Line of Fate may also rise from the Mount of Venus inside the Line of Life. Such a position indicates that passionate love will affect one's whole career, and these people will usually place their affections on someone who is married or otherwise unable to return the love they give.

Next you need to look at where the Line of Fate terminates. It may end early or continue all the way to the base of the middle finger, indicating lifelong direction.

As with the case of any line, the Line of Fate may stop at another line, may suddenly disappear (terminate), or may gradually fade out. Each case shows the focus of the career and its probable termination. (A line that suddenly ends or is cut off may still appear farther along the palm, so look to see if it reappears on its natural path after a large break.) When the Line of Fate is stopped by the Line of Head, it gives the promise of success thwarted by a mental blunder or poor choices. When stopped by the Line of Heart, success is ruined by the affections. When stopped by a separate unattached line, the success of the individual will be stopped by the single situation represented by that line.

The Mount of Saturn is the normal place for the Line of Fate to end. This gives the person a serious nature in regard to career. Should it end on any other mount, the direction of the career will be toward the aspects of that mount.

If the Line of Fate joins another line and both proceed together, this shows a blending of the career with the energy represented by the joining line. The direction the blended line continues in is the direction taken by the life and career.

Breaks or changes in the Line of Fate indicate breaks or changes in the person's career or residence. (Changes in a line refers to cases where a single clear line suddenly shows several finer lines in place of the clear one or when the line itself goes in a different direction.)

LINE OF SUCCESS

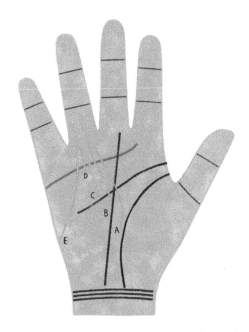

The Line of Success (also known as the Line of Apollo) is an often misinterpreted line in palmistry. Each person's view of success is different, and this line reflects these differing views as well as the achievements with their own particular brand of success.

The Line of Success is a modifier of the Line of Fate, so anything seen on this line must be verified with the Line of Fate. The Line of Success, when present, may rise from as low as the Mount of Pluto or may start above the Line of Heart.

Rising from the Line of Life (A), it shows success in artistic pursuits and an admiration of all beautiful things. From the Line of Fate (B), this increases the success promised by the Line of Fate and gives distinction to the person. Rising from the Line of Head (C), the success of the subject will be hard-earned and by their own efforts alone. From the Line of Heart (D), it shows that the distinction and recognition so dearly desired will not come until late in life. From the Mount of Luna (E), this placement indicates that one's success will not be by their own merits but is largely dependent on the help of others. (This is a common placement on the hands of poets and fiction authors.)

On a hand with a deep hollow or a poorly formed Line of Head, the Line of Success loses all power. In these cases, it shows that the success promised will not be attained due to the circumstances indicated elsewhere on the hands.

When the line moves straight on its natural path toward the base of the ring finger, the success shown is in artistic endeavors and the creation and sharing of beauty. This line can also bend slightly near its end, toward either the middle or little finger. Wherever any line terminates shows the natural direction and motivation of that line's energy. A Line of Success bending toward the middle finger takes on the Saturnian aspects. Successes are in more serious and academic endeavors. When the line bends toward the base of the little finger, Mercurial traits such as commerce and quick thinking are the natural talents.

The complete absence of a Line of Success indicates that while these people may work hard and be deserving of honor and fame, they are unlikely to achieve any worldly recognition.

LINE OF HEALTH

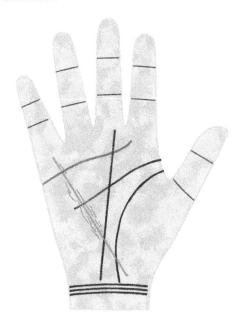

The Line of Health (also called Hepatica Line or Mercury Line) indicates the basic health of the individual and the type of health problems they may encounter. It is an excellent sign to be without this line entirely; it shows that there is no interaction between sickness and health. The person maintains a robust and healthy constitution. Any time the Line of Health is present, it warns of a delicate point of health and an area of potential concern.

The line should run straight down the hand; the straighter the better. If there is more than one line present at any given point, each line is indicative of another area of health concern. Quite often, you will find many small lines exerting their influence at once, each showing a different difficulty in the health.

The isolation of health conditions with regard to palmistry is an in-depth study in itself and is beyond the scope of this book. As a beginner, if you have a Line of Health or identify one on someone you are doing a reading for, simply remember the steps we all need to take to maintain optimal health and well-being.

CHAPTER

7

MINOR PALM LINES

G enerally speaking, any horizontal mark on the palm is considered a block or challenge to overcome. Any vertical mark is considered an advancement or a characteristic that propels the individual to further develop their personality. In addition to this general rule, there are numerous specific markings that can be interpreted according to the area or mount on which they are found. These specific markings, in addition to the minor lines, provide a more complete analysis of the hands and their meaning. As with all other markings, no one sign can be taken as conclusive. Each one provides one more piece of the puzzle.

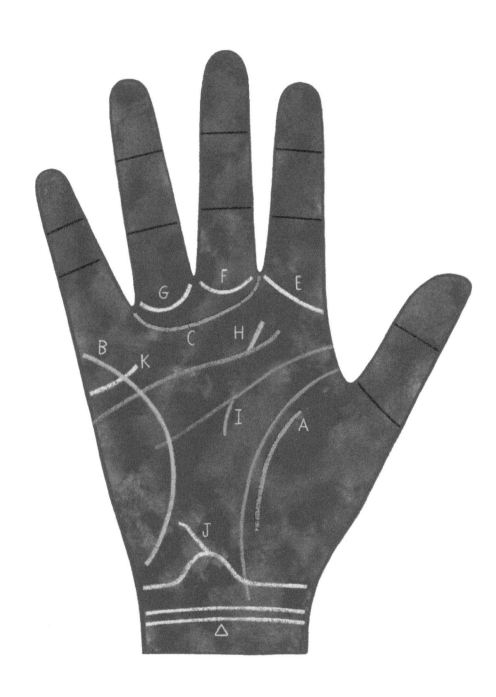

Minor Lines and Other Markings

The minor lines are considered less significant than the major lines, but it is still important to examine them when doing a reading. Minor lines and specific markings can be attached to major lines or be completely independent. They are always interpreted according to the mount or area on which they are found.

LINE OF MARS

The Line of Mars (A), also called "the inner line of life," does not appear on all hands. Contrary to what the name implies, it appears on the Mount of Venus. When present, it adds strength to the Line of Life, allowing the person to overcome apparently insurmountable odds—often strong family interference. When there is a break in the Line of Life, the Line of Mars acts as a buffer, backing up the life force energy to avoid some of the negative impact of the broken line.

LINE OF INTUITION

The Line of Intuition (B) denotes exactly that—the person has senses and impressions that cannot be rationally explained. When found on a square palm with few lines, the individual dismisses these intuitions as just imagination. Seen on a hand with many lines and long fingers, the person tends to rely on their heightened intuition more and more frequently and with increasing accuracy. Asked how they came to their conclusions, they are not able to say, only that they "feel it." This is a somewhat common line on the hands of psychics and spiritual mediums.

GIRDLE OF VENUS

Traditional palmistry holds that the Girdle of Venus (C) indicates promiscuity and excess affections. While this can be the case on strong hands with very few lines, it does not often appear this way. Much more frequently, the Girdle of Venus is seen on palms that show a multitude of fine lines. In these cases, the Girdle of Venus only amplifies the nervous and worrying temperament denoted by the many lines.

BRACELETS

There are typically three lines running across the wrist, known as the bracelets (D). As with other lines, the optimum appearance is to be clearly marked and without any crossing lines. The Bracelet Lines can rise in the middle toward the center of the palm and be chained rather than clearly marked. This tends to indicate difficulty conceiving children, as does the absence of one of the three bracelets.

RING OF SOLOMON

The Ring of Solomon (E) is a small line rising from between the index and middle finger, sweeps into the Mount of Jupiter and ends near or on the Line of Life. On all hands, it indicates an interest in psychology and a love of learning. If a strong Line of Head is also present, the person has a natural talent in occult subjects and is likely to attain a strong degree of mastery in these fields.

RING OF SATURN

The Ring of Saturn (F) is typically considered an unfortunate mark. It loops under or through the Mount of Saturn, effectively cutting off the energy flow of the Line of Fate to the fingertip. People with this line usually have little patience for a long career and jump from one occupation to another. The middle finger is the finger of balance in the personality, so a ring underneath it reflects the tendency toward a strong imbalance in motivations and efforts. Goals may be lofty, but the steady work to achieve them cannot be maintained for long.

RING OF APOLLO

The Ring of Apollo (G) is another line that appears only infrequently on the palms. Just as the Rings of Solomon and Saturn arc around the bases of the index and middle fingers respectively, the Ring of Apollo curves underneath the ring finger (Apollo finger), serving to "cut off" the artistic expressions of creativity and beauty. Although it usually appears on a large Mount of Apollo, the creative drive and talents are not easily expressed due to other priorities and responsibilities in the person's life. When the Ring of Apollo, however, is cut by a deep vertical line going through it, the individual has learned to overcome this creative suppression and prioritizes their need for artistry and beauty in all activities.

ASCENDING AND DESCENDING BRANCHES

Branches are lines of weaker strength and depth than the line they originate from. Branches can be ascending (moving toward the fingers) (H) or descending (moving toward the wrist) (I). They help join and blend the original line with aspects of the mount they connect it to. When a branch is ascending, it indicates a slight weakening of the main line, resulting in an overall improvement or advancement that propels the person forward. When descending, the slight weakening of the line reflects additional challenges to overcome.

TRAVEL LINES

Ascending branches from the uppermost Bracelet line are known as Travel Lines (J). These do not actually indicate voyages, but rather an innate curiosity and adventurous spirit. With this love of new experiences, it is natural for the person to travel great distances given the opportunity. In traditional palmistry, Travel Lines are considered to be the small lines on the little finger side of the hand. These, however, are actually lines relating to health.

LINE OF MARRIAGE

The Line of Marriage (K) does not represent the actual ceremony of marriage, but rather shows an emotional bond that might well be called a "soul mate." Without the presence of this line, there is no single love in the person's life, this being eliminated in favor of universal love.

The Line of Marriage should be clear, straight, and without obstruction of any kind. Only long lines relate to marriage; shorter lines refer to liaisons or marriage contemplated. To read this line more clearly, pull the little finger outward away from the rest of the fingers.

The placement of the line will show the approximate age at which the relationship will begin. Appearing near the Line of Heart, it indicates age 14 to 21. Halfway up the Mount of Mercury is ages 21 to 28. Three-quarters of the way up is 28 to 35.

It is quite common to see more than one Line of Marriage. The same rules apply to each one, or each relationship. By comparing the depth and clarity of each line, you can determine which is the strongest relationship. A Line of Marriage ending with a wide fork usually indicates a separation of the relationship or divorce.

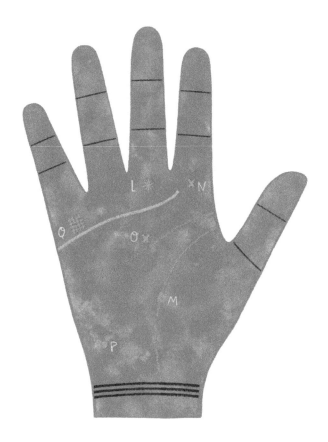

THE STAR

Three or more lines intersecting at a single point is known as the Star (L). It is traditionally viewed as a very promising sign, indicating success or riches. With three separate lines interacting, the Star exerts an influence that proves nearly impossible to escape. As with all other markings, it is favorable or unfavorable depending on your point of view. It can be viewed as "too much of a good thing."

On the Mount of Mercury, the Star promises success in commerce, but usually to the exclusion of love relationships. On the Mount of Apollo, it denotes great financial success, but without the joy and emotional fulfillment. On the Mount of Jupiter, there is the achievement of ambitions but with little satisfaction.

Stars on the Mount of Saturn are the most notable. It shows an unrivalled distinction in the career efforts, but at a great cost. People with this mark are almost playthings of fate, and life seems to have cast them for one special role. The unfortunate part is that their success is usually short lived. The expression "King for a day, but crowned with doom" tends to apply here.

Stars may also appear on the side of a mount. In these cases, the person is associated with and influenced by someone who has the achievement and distinction, but they will not be as successful themselves.

Stars can also appear on the fingertips, revealing the proverbial "Midas Touch" in one area of life. While the Star gives the promise of distinction, what kind of distinction and its impact are influenced by the remainder of the hand. Promise does not come to fruition without the appropriate effort.

THE SQUARE

The Square (M) is commonly referred to as the "mark of preservation" and often appears surrounding part of one of the major lines. Although it does indicate difficulties in life, it is as if those troubles happen all around the individual rather than affecting them directly. A Square surrounding breaks in a line serves as a buffer of sorts, still showing difficulties but with the impact greatly lessened.

THE CROSS

The Cross (N) is simply the impact of two lines interacting at right angles or in opposition to each other. It is in all cases a challenge and indicates that the influence of both lines is being applied to a single area in life. A compromise of some sort is always necessary.

The Cross can appear anywhere on the hand and may be formed by the crossing of other lines or can appear clearly on its own. In either case, it means the same thing: Two opposing areas of life will come into conflict, and some sort of compromise will be needed.

The most notable placement for the Cross is on the Mount of Jupiter. This is viewed as a very favorable mark in traditional palmistry, for it shows a moment of greatness when successes go far toward satisfying the ambitions. The conflict or compromise here is that with high success comes the tendency to "rest on one's laurels," thereby achieving far less than would otherwise be possible. There's been great achievement but it could be greater with continued effort.

THE CROIX MYSTIQUE

The Croix Mystique (also called Mystic Cross) (O) is of particular importance when it occurs, since its placement is at the very center of the hand. It has traditionally stood for a belief or ability in the occult arts. What must be understood is that these arts included medicine, astronomy, astrology, prediction, psychology, religion, and other areas of "secret knowledge." The Croix Mystique signifies an understanding and insight into the intricate patterns of life.

The closer the Croix Mystique is to the Line of the Heart, the more this understanding will take the form of superstition. Lying closer to the Line of Head, it takes the form of occult abilities. In cases where the Croix Mystique is formed by the Line of Fate, occult matters will be prominent throughout one's career.

THE CIRCLE

The Circle (P) can appear anywhere on the hand. These circular marks denote a sense of "going around in circles" without change. Circles tend to indicate areas of frustration and resentment. A Circle is traditionally considered to be a positive sign that shows achievement and success, but for some people, their continued success in a single area becomes monotonous and exhausting.

THE GRILL

The Grill (Q) is the crossing of many blocks and advancements. Too many conflicting influences converge on a single area, so the person is predisposed to the negative traits represented by the mount on which it appears.

Condition of the Lines

The condition of the lines, and not merely their placement and direction, is of utmost importance to the analysis. The optimum appearance of the lines is deep, clean, light red, and with no apparent breaks or other markings. This indicates someone who is active and robust with a hopeful disposition. Remember to factor in that individuals with darker skin naturally have darker lines than individuals with lighter skin.

Lines appearing yellow denote a proud yet reserved nature. The lines may also appear very dark in color, almost black. People with this coloration typically have a grave disposition, are rather haughty, and prone to unforgiveness and revenge.

When reading the lines, also take into account that the strength of any given line (its depth and clarity) is modified by the number of lines appearing on the hand. The person with a multitude of fine lines across the entire palm is nervous and worries about things that are of no consequence to anyone else. It takes several agreeing marks to significantly influence such people.

Hands with only a few lines are well defined and easily read. Every line is of great significance, so only one or two well-marked signs might indicate a near certainty of its validity.

Tips for Reading the Lines

There are a few techniques that can help you identify the lines and their characteristics more clearly:

- Press on the line with your thumb and then observe it as soon as you release the pressure. A line that is growing stronger (increasing in influence) will become much clearer and more distinct for a second or two after you stop pressing on it. A line that is fading out will have almost disappeared after pressing on it, showing that its influence is fading.

- Have the person being analyzed open and close their hands several times quickly. This helps to relax the muscles so you can read the natural state more easily. Shaking the hands and fingers vigorously also works.

- Put the hands under good lighting. LED light using the white spectrum is the most effective of all types of illumination. LED flashlights are inexpensive and can be an essential part of any complete analysis.

- Photograph or scan the palms, and then use a black marker on the printout to trace over the lines you are sure of. By looking at these darkened lines, you may be able to see and identify the remainder of unclear lines.

PART
three

THE ART OF
PALM READING

CHAPTER
8

HOW *to* NAVIGATE
a READING

Palmistry and hand analysis are every bit an art as they are a science. These skills require both knowledge and practice. Too many readers simply repeat what they have been taught or read without any real understanding of how the different parts interact with each other to create the larger picture. Be careful not to take what you read at face value without considering all aspects of the details. As a beginner, flip through this book as much as you need to during a reading to take everything you see into consideration.

Remember that the information you can read from the hands by no means indicates permanent traits. Movements and gestures change as quickly as the thoughts and emotions. Some of the hand shapes will change over the years. Even the lines themselves can grow longer or fade out with the passage of time and even quicker when a paradigm shift occurs. The one exception is the dermatoglyphics, which, as you learned, are fingerprints and the similar patterns; these were present before you were born and stay the same throughout life.

Enchanting Preparations

The first few minutes of a reading are perhaps the most important. If you approach it poorly (for example, being outwardly nervous and making excuses for yourself or shaking a hand too firmly or roughly grabbing the hands for examination), the person you are reading for can become uncomfortable and their hands will not show accurate movements and positions for interpretation. But when you approach it well, you can read the person's natural movements and help them stay relaxed and calm.

Therefore, the first step in preparing for a reading is to approach it with the right physical and mental state. Calmness in both mind and body is necessary if you want any degree of accuracy. Physical stress (such as right after a heavy workout) or any unresolved anxiety you feel can completely alter the way you interpret what you see and read.

Before I interpret anyone's hands, including my own, I follow a simple routine to prepare. First, I do a Zen one-point meditation to clear my mind and body, and follow that up with a meditation that is Shaolin in origin to draw in vital energy. After that, I take a relaxed, slow walk. Some readers like to use crystals, yoga, or candles and incense to achieve a state of calmness. For many, chanting the "Jewel of the Lotus" mantra (*om mani padme hum*) works extremely well on its own in preparation for a reading. As a beginner to palm reading, I encourage you to prepare your mind with whatever calming methods you find most comfortable.

Before and after each reading, wash and/or sanitize your hands. The person you are reading for does not necessarily need to wash their hands after getting their hands read, but it still makes sense for simple hygiene reasons. The important part is for you, as the reader, to clear yourself of others' residual energy before beginning a new reading. I prefer washing with very cold water for this purpose.

When you start a reading, especially as a beginner, remind yourself that we all have freedom of choice in life. You need never fear "bad" signs or markings. As long as there is breath in the lungs, there is the opportunity for change. While this is true for everyone, I do not recommend saying this aloud until well into the reading. Your calmness will help the person you are reading for be more relaxed and help you deliver any "negative" information in the best way possible. Querents are looking for answers, and I've found that they are often looking for their choices to be made for them. They may also hold the view that they have no need to change, thinking, "This is just the way I am." By delaying the statement that we all have freedom of choice, you are first providing them with some information to work with and ponder.

Reading Hands

One of the first questions asked by many beginners is "Which hand do you read?" Some prefer to look at only the dominant palm, but this can lead to a great deal of information being omitted, so I encourage you to observe both the dominant and nondominant palms for the most accurate reading.

The first thing to do is determine which hand is naturally dominant. I have found the best way to do this is to put both palms together and carefully line them up at the wrist. Then align the thumbs. Next look to the lines separating the finger segments and place the bottom segment lines together. In most people, you will find that the dominant hand is slightly larger, visible by the overall length of the fingers.

It is very important to look at both the front and back of the dominant and nondominant hands. On the backs of the hands, you are looking for cuts, scrapes, or other injuries and any chance markings.

The general rule is that markings on the palm side show the more personal information meant for yourself, while the back of the hands shows information readily visible to others even when you attempt to hide it.

READING DOMINANT HANDS

Right-hand dominance occurs in more than 85 percent of people. Only 10 to 11 percent of the population is left-handed. The remaining 4 to 5 percent are partially or completely ambidextrous (able to use both hands equally well). Given these percentages, if you have any doubt as to which hand is dominant, ask the person you are reading. If this information is not available (as with a small child, for instance), choose the right hand.

The dominant hand is traditionally viewed as "the hand we make for ourselves." It reflects the more prominent traits in both personality and in health. You can't simply ignore the other hand, however. Variations in the lines and other markings between the hands show some of the strongest influences in an individual's life.

The dominant hand reveals where the person applies their efforts in pursuit of their goals and ambitions. It shows their fortune, if you will, for both positive and negative influences and probable outcomes. It is also more accurate in determining weak or difficult areas where there are still challenges to be overcome.

READING NONDOMINANT HANDS

In traditional palmistry, the nondominant hand is known as "the hand you were born with." It shows latent talents and characteristics. Basically, every option you had when you were born is marked there.

On most hands, you will see many more lines on the nondominant hand compared to the dominant. This shows how the person has developed their personality in a manner that has then made them much calmer and more determined than they would have been without their consistently applied efforts toward their goals.

When the nondominant hand is seen with fewer lines and the dominant has many fine lines across it, this indicates that the person is more anxious than would otherwise be normal for them had they kept more focus on positive mental and physical activities. They can still incorporate these activities to reduce their anxiety. For them, some form of meditation to discipline the mind is required. (Yoga and tai chi are two excellent methods that are often overlooked as possible forms of meditation.)

COMPARING PALMS

I recommend reading both hands, although you can still read them singularly. However, when you ignore one of the hands, what you will get is either an interpretation that looks only at potentials or one that sees choices that have already been made along with their probable outcomes. Reading and comparing both palms gives you a bigger-picture perspective.

At times, you will find a potential or probable difficulty coming into someone's life as indicated on the dominant hand. Examine the same areas of the nondominant to see what potentials could be tapped and developed to help modify or overcome the challenge.

As mentioned earlier, when analyzing cuts, injuries, and other anomalies, those found on the nondominant hand typically reflect relationships with family members. These markings on the dominant hand indicate themselves and their shorter-term relationships.

Conducting a Reading

When doing a reading, start the analysis before you even look at the palms. Your first step is to merely observe the general characteristics of the hands. Say nothing of what you see at the beginning. You can gain a general understanding of the person well before going into any kind of detail. Look for traits that agree with or contradict each other. If you note several signs noting very similar things, that trait is a near certainty and a likely foundation point in the person's life. Contradictory but well-marked signs identify the person's unique challenges and the duality of their nature.

STEP 1: HAND MOVEMENTS

First, look to the normal movements of the hands and fingers. Do they wave about, showing a more anxious person, or do they stay relatively stationary, telling of a calmer, firmer demeanor? Are the thumbs held outside the hand or contracted and sitting inside the closed fingers? As opposed to the thumb outside the hand, the contracted thumb identifies someone with less willpower to make changes on their own and tend to rely more on the strength of others.

STEP 2: HAND POSITIONS

Look to see how the person naturally holds their hands even before you start the reading. Do they immediately and excitedly put both palms face up in front of you or keep the palms hidden from your view? Some people are naturally more cautious and secretive than others, while some become that way only during the reading (usually as a way of testing your abilities). The more they hide their hands and palms, the more cautious and secretive they are about the reading. Hidden palms will offer far less information on their own and will take careful observation and questioning. Hands in the pockets show a reluctance to share personal information.

STEP 3: GAINING THEIR TRUST

The majority of people you read for will be more than a bit nervous or anxious when you begin, even when they don't show it outwardly. Take this opportunity to remain calm yourself, gently taking both hands in yours and turning them palm side up and then palms down. You are looking for strong anomalies, but more important, you are allowing them to become relaxed and ready to listen.

It is usually at this stage when the person will tell you of any specific concerns they have or their personal motivations for getting their hands read in the first place. For some, it is merely general interest, seeing what the hands can reveal. Others may have very specific reasons, seeking just one or two specific details relating to their life or current choices they face. Both are equally valid, and you as a palmist need to respect their needs and choice.

STEP 4: CHEIROGNOMY

Identify the basic hand type from the Four Elements, and then look to the finger lengths and fingertips. Compare both hands with palms together to see if there is a noticeably dominant one. Note the fingernails, looking to see if they are all the same type or are mixed between two or more categories.

Now check the flexibility of all four fingers and the thumb on each hand. Are they fixed or rigid? Does the thumb bend back easily or feel as if it would break before bending? At this point, look at the skin texture and thickness, and any sideways bending of the fingers at the knuckles. Next, examine the mounts of the palms. Note which ones are elevated, flat, or depressed. Which mount is the largest and firmest? Are any of the mounts soft and flabby?

After these four steps, you should have a good understanding of the person's basic character and motivations. Now you can move on to reading the lines.

STEP 5: CHEIROMANCY, MAJOR LINES

Look first at the Line of Head. Note whether it starts inside the Line of Life, attached to it, or below it on the Mount of Inner Mars. Next see where the lines progress and where it ends. Does it show the practical and logical aspects when ending on the Mount of Outer Mars or sweep down to the Mount of Luna or Neptune, denoting a consistently active imagination?

Examine the condition and color of the Line of Head. Note the appearance and placement of any breaks or other significant markings.

The Line of Heart comes next. Again, look at the start location, ending, color, consistency, and all other well-marked signs. If you didn't already notice it in step 3, check for the presence of the Simian Line. A joined Line of Head and Line of Heart running straight across the palm affects every part of the personality, adding focus and intensity to all their efforts.

Then factor in the Line of Life. Is it clear and deeply marked, showing the physical strength and endurance to act on motivations? Or is the line made up of many small lines, or have a chained appearance full of islands or breaks? These show that the physical energy is at least at times insufficient to follow their goals. Examine whether the Line of Life makes a large arc extending well into the palm (showing a strongly extroverted nature) or if the line makes a small arc going a third of the way across the palm (showing the introvert).

Continue by examining the Lines of Fate, Success, and Health. Out of those three lines, I prefer examination in their order of deepest marked or most anomalies first. This gives you the more constant factors or biggest contradictions before looking at each line in general only.

STEP 6: CHEIROMANCY, THE MINOR LINES

Finally, look to the minor lines and individual markings, starting with the Line of Mars. This line does not appear on all hands, so whenever it does, it is significant. Check to see if there is a Ring of Solomon, Saturn, or Apollo.

Only after all these examinations should you look at the individual markings such as the Circle, Cross, Grill, and Star. Remember that agreeing marks and signs strengthen their influence in the personality, while contradictory signs show conflict and compromise.

Changing Hands

Your hands can and will change slightly over time. These changes show how one's life path has been altered due to personal choices and the use of willpower.

Many of our major life events are shown clearly on the hands and can be divined through palmistry analysis. It is our life choices, however, that create and influence these events. Willpower and self-determination have far more influence on our major life events than any predestination or fate.

Not all changes on the hands are dramatic alterations on the line placements. Most of what you will see is far more subtle. Minor changes in line color occur on an almost hourly basis. Read what you see. As long as a marking is visible, it has influence. Exercise can make the lines darker or redder. Alcohol can give the palms a mottled appearance.

For the long term, the best way to track and record the ongoing changes on your hands is to take photographs or scans of both hands every six months or so. Compare these past and present images to see if willpower and applied efforts have successfully made positive changes or if lack of responsibility and idleness has created additional difficulties.

CHAPTER

9

DIVINING POWERFUL INSIGHTS

I t is time to put everything you've learned into practice. Palmistry is not just about reading markings on the hands and relaying those details. How the information is conveyed is equally important. It is all for naught if the reading changes nothing.

The satisfaction you can gain from helping others better their own lives can be tremendous and is just as satisfying as the feelings you get from improving your own circumstances. To get there, however, you need a degree of empathy and understanding. You will also need to ask questions, whether of yourself or others.

Reading Your Querent

Ultimately, there is no such thing as a good or bad sign in palmistry. It all comes down to the interaction of all the markings, and the querent's own perspective. If a person desires a deep and lasting love relationship above all things, a strong limitation to their career achievements caused by excessive romantic efforts can be viewed by them as very positive, even though their vocational potential is cut short. A person's excessive internalized anger that causes premature illness might be seen as powerfully positive if this same anger motivates them to achieve otherwise impossible goals.

A thorough examination of the hands can provide some context as to how they see and prioritize conflicting motivations, but you will still have to ask direct questions to understand their personal bias and the things they hold most dear. Even if the rest of the world agrees that a trait or behavior is negative and strongly limits or shortens a person's life, their own personal perspective and beliefs are still to be considered "right."

The first question to ask is always "Is there anything specific you are wanting to learn from this reading?" Their need might seem inconsequential or petty to you, or even show that they are avoiding their real issues. If you don't answer a specific question that is their priority, they are likely to discount most of what you say and seek their answers elsewhere. Yes, when there are more important issues to be dealt with, then definitely discuss those. But always be sure to present your interpretation of what the hands say about the querent's most pressing concern.

If you cannot find an answer to a querent's specific question, just admit that fact to them. Share what you can see without guessing or embellishment. Honesty is of paramount importance in palmistry, and anything but complete honesty can quickly destroy your own reputation as well as others' confidence in you.

HOW TO VIEW "GOOD" AND "BAD" SIGNS

We all have a role to play in this world. Morals and ethics depend completely on personal viewpoints and experiences. We all have different paths to walk, and different ways to influence others and our environment. As it is written in the *Tao Te Ching*, "When all the world recognizes beauty as beauty, this in itself is ugliness." No single belief or motivation can ever be considered right or wrong for everyone. In fact, in accepting these differences, we come to understand life more fully and grow both individually and as a species.

Because of this dependence on experience and perspective, there is one rule in palmistry that comes before all others: *do not judge*. It is not for the palmist to remove a person from their chosen path, nor to steer them toward your own personal beliefs. To view your querent as good, bad, right, or wrong is the worst mistake you can make, both for them and for yourself.

You might find a strong and clear Line of Life that is marred and weakened by an average Line of Head, accompanied by a dominant Mount of Saturn with spatulate fingertips. You could ask this person, "Why do you feel the need to develop your intellect and scholarly learning at the cost of your own health, perhaps even shortening your own life?" Asking for details and perspectives in this way is usually well-received by the querent. They recognize and appreciate the accuracy of the suggested interpretation and rarely get defensive or angry because they see that you hold no judgment for or against their priorities and life choices. You are simply reading "what is."

With injuries or amputations, it is best to give only a basic interpretation of it at first, and then ask them when and how the injury occurred and what their mind-set was at the time. This allows you to put yourself in their shoes somewhat and understand the importance to them of their motivations and choices. My father lost both of his hands when he was a teenager. This would typically be viewed as a terrible thing, but as a result of his accident, I got involved in studying the hands and made it my professional and personal focus. Perhaps some things in life are preordained or predestined, and perhaps not. Certainly either belief is absurd, for our limited understanding prevents anyone from knowing the absolute truth for sure.

Remember that everyone lies, both to themselves and to others. When you are getting uncomfortably close to a difficult truth in your analysis for someone, it is a natural response for the person to become at least somewhat defensive. People will usually put a positive spin on the question in their responses, although some may be self-deprecating or express guilt. All of these are normal responses; accept them for what they are.

Reading Your Own Hands

It can be difficult to remain objective when reading our own hands. We tend to have very firm and fixed opinions about our motivations and desires, and have a difficult time challenging these beliefs. This can be especially true for those who have done a great deal of soul searching. In challenging our beliefs, we are also challenging whether the years of efforts and self-examination were worth it or a waste of time in our own views.

When reading yourself, try to step back from viewing the interpretation as part of who you are. Your personal biases and fixed beliefs not only make an accurate analysis difficult, but they can also cause you to learn inaccurate assessments that will affect how you read the hands of others. If your interpretation seems grossly inaccurate, ask a friend if it seems correct to them. You might be surprised, because the way we see ourselves is different from the way others view us.

Read your own hands exactly as you would if they were someone else's. Don't take shortcuts by thinking, "This line on my palm must mean such and such because I know that is who I am." This method of reading your hands as if they were someone else's also has the benefit of helping you understand how and why others might become defensive or disagree with your analysis of them.

Remember to ask yourself questions as well. Frequently remind yourself, "If I saw this on another person's hands, what would I ask them?" Don't be surprised when many of these questions are some of the toughest ones you will ever get. It is difficult to view ourselves without our personal-bias filters. By following this technique, you will learn to be less judgmental of yourself and your actions and choices.

Divining with Sensitivity and Sympathy

I know I've said it before, but it is important to remember that the lines and markings indicating our future are subject to some degree of change. Sometimes it takes a constant effort, while at other times it can be changed with a single paradigm shift. Likewise, marks indicating past events can fade as we lessen the event's influence in our present and future.

Used well, palmistry is not a predictive tool but rather a method of gaining insight into our nature and our path in life. It can be looked at as reading the book of our life, from conception through to death. This book on our hands, however, keeps being edited and some chapters even get rewritten. Don't read your hands to see if you are the hero or villain in your story. At times, we have all been both. Much like meditation, palmistry cannot be forced into what we might want at the time.

Compassion is an integral part of any good hand reading. We all have our glories, and we all have our traumas. It's not the event itself that matters, but rather the impact the event has in our life. One person might feel traumatized by not getting a sports car for their 16th birthday, while for someone else it could take fully breaking their will and spirit to count as a trauma. You may not feel that an event could be important in influencing someone's future or even that it could be remotely significant. Without compassion, we naturally compare an individual's difficulties against the identical challenge for others. With compassion, we see that it is never about just the event, but about the trauma's influence in one's life.

Be sure to use this same tolerance when reading your own hands. The more you judge your hands and yourself as inadequate, the more you will judge others in the same way. After all, whose version of "success" or "trauma" could ever be correct for anyone but themselves?

Use your knowledge of hand reading to learn from the past, live in the present, and put your efforts toward the future you want.

Putting It All Together

You are now able to combine and integrate all the separate branches of hand analysis you have learned. Start with cheirognomy to understand the basic character and motivations, and then add in the cheiromancy to read the "book of life." Look for multiple confirming signs for a single trait or event, and also any contradictory markings that are well-marked. Only when you factor in both of these can you understand the life and person written on the hands.

It is normal to have a great many difficult or challenging signs present at the same time on the hands. Typically, one challenge or poor marking influences or leads to another, which leads to the next, then the next, and so on.

Think of all the different difficult marks as a row of dominoes. If the first domino is not pushed over (the first obstacle not overcome), then all of the dominoes will never fall. More challenges will continually be added, requiring endless effort and still not overcoming them all. By identifying and dealing with the primary challenge, or root cause, all of the dominoes will fall. This does not mean that you only have to deal with just one issue. When the first difficulty is faced and overcome, it will naturally lead to the next one in line to become prominent, and require its own introspection and effort.

Because every pair of hands is unique, there is unfortunately no prewritten script or specific order of interpretation you can follow when doing a palmistry reading. Look for what stands out, especially in the minor lines and individual markings. Important signs will almost scream at you to take notice of them.

When presenting your findings, it is best to use language and terminology that is comfortable for the person hearing it. It is easier for people to follow general and commonly used names than it is for them to understand arcane or medical jargon. What is important is for them to clearly understand the facts you are trying to deliver. For example, it is easier to follow "hand bones" and "finger bones" than it is to grasp "metacarpals" and "phalanges." Speak to their level wherever you can.

The blank hand template on page 112 can help you learn from and record what you see in the hands. The majority of people will be reluctant to allow you to take high-quality photos or scans of their hands but will readily accept you drawing the information you see on a template. By drawing each important sign you see, you can more easily spot which challenges are the most important at that time.

I used these blanks in almost all my readings for many years. They not only aid in seeing where conflicts and confirmations occur, but also drawing on blank templates helps you remember specific details you want to bring up during your analysis. Without writing them down, it is easy to forget important details that might influence the entire interpretation.

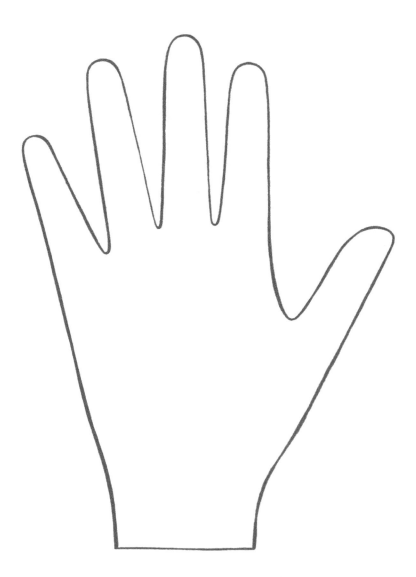

Putting Insight into Action

After having a palm reading done, it is normal to have an emotional reaction that can last for a few days. Optimally the emotional response is one of inspiration and empowerment. The reaction, however, can also be anger, resentment, or anxiety. Remind the person (who might be yourself) that the time to take action based on their analysis is within these first few days. After that, the newly found motivation will fade.

Whether the emotional response is positive or negative, this is the time to take goal-oriented action. Use the new understanding and motivation to begin the steps required to improve the circumstances. Then, even years of required effort can come easily.

Anxious responses usually occur when there is an indicator of poor health, relationship difficulties, or financial concerns. Just take at least that first step and the rest will fall into place naturally. Do whatever is indicated from the palmistry analysis. The key is not to try to overcome the difficulty all at once, but only to take that first step.

Positive emotional reactions tend to happen when the person is able to give themselves permission to finally seek the improvements they have been wanting in their lives. This sense of empowerment can fade all too quickly, however, so it is again important to take the first step that leads to continued action. Whatever the desire, the first few days after a reading is the time to start.

CONCLUSION
The Path of the Palmist

Congratulations to you for persevering and continuing your study of the hands and how to analyze them. At this point, you may be starting to look at hands differently, picking up information from just a cursory glance. Keep observing the hands of others during your regular conversations and interactions. You will be surprised at just how quickly you become adept at noticing personality traits and how they are expressed.

If you wish to advance your study of palm reading, an area you will want to examine is dermatoglyphics, especially the fingerprint patterns and placements. Understanding these fine markings will greatly expand your ability to interpret the rest of the hands. It is a detailed study, however, and one that cannot be rushed through. The Resources section includes a few great places to start.

What motivated you to study palmistry and what else interests you about the hands? By following your own interests, you will find the learning process faster and more enjoyable. Do you want to develop hand analysis into a part- or full-time career? It takes quite some time to gain the skill level necessary, but the pay can be far better than many other vocations. You may need to study business and promotion if you don't already have proficiency in these areas. Website development and social media would also aid you in moving from amateur to professional.

One of my favorite branches of palmistry is cheirokinesics, the movements of the hands. It can be somewhat difficult to learn because there is so little information written on the subject. You would need at least some training in basic psychology. Watching the hands of actors on television and in movies is a great way to practice, since many use "method acting" to get into character.

If meditation is of interest to you, you might enjoy studying the multitudes of specific hand positions for meditations in many different fields. One of the great benefits in this subject is the mental focus, calmness, and internal power that it gives with practice. Breath control is essential, so if you have already developed that through your other interests (swimming, rock climbing, aerobics, or playing wind instruments), you will be able to do the meditations yourself rather than just learning the theory.

Reflexology and palmar massage are other areas you could choose to delve into. Each of these is greatly improved by an understanding of palmistry. Whatever your interests and however you choose to pursue your studies in palmistry, know that everything you learn will help benefit you in your life, understanding your own life path, and becoming more at one with the universe.

RESOURCES

Cheiro's Language of the Hand by Cheiro

This book isn't very long nor in-depth, but it is still considered one of the classics of modern palm reading. Although Cheiro's original manuscript was printed in 1900 and is no longer available, a compilation was first published 50 years later and the information is just as valid today.

The Benham Book of Palmistry by William G. Benham

First published in 1900, Benham's work on explaining hand reading is still one of the most complete, accurate, and detailed books on the subject. It does take some interpretation and tolerance to convert many old terms to their modern counterparts.

Encyclopedia of Palmistry by Ed Campbell

This 1996 work by Ed Campbell covers a detailed and nearly complete analysis of the hands. Campbell is considered by many to be the most achieved and acclaimed historian on the subject who still follows and incorporates modern research studies.

www.ModernHandReadingForum.com

Developed and overseen by Martijn van Mensvoort in the Netherlands, this website has become the undisputed hub for online learning and discussion of all aspects of palmistry. The sheer volume of information it contains and the number of active users can make it a bit difficult to navigate, and even harder to leave the site once you start reading.

GodGivenGlyphs.com

Jennifer Hirsch has been providing hand readings and instruction for decades. She is one of the best to learn from as a beginner or advanced student.

REFERENCES

Benham, William G. *The Benham Book of Palmistry: The Essential Work*. 10th ed. Hollywood, CA: Newcastle Publishing Company, 1988.

Campbell, Edward D. *The Encyclopedia of Palmistry*. 1st ed. London, UK: Robert Hale Ltd, 2007.

Cheiro. *Cheiro's Guide to the Hand: A Practical Work on the Sciences of Cheirognomy and Cheiromancy from a Useful and Scientific Standpoint Based on the System and Experience of Chiero*. 1st ed. Chicago, IL: Rand, McNally & Co., 1900.

Cheiro. *Cheiro's Language of the Hand: The Classic of Palmistry*. Upper Saddle River, NJ: Prentice Hall PTR, 1987.

Encyclopedia.com. "Cheirological Society of Great Britain (Dukes)." *Encyclopedia of Occultism and Parapsychology*. Accessed August 26, 2019. www.encyclopedia.com/science/encyclopedias -almanacs-transcripts-and-maps/cheirological-society-great -britain-dukes.

Holtzman, Arnold. *Biometric Definitions of Personality*. 3rd ed. Accessed August 30, 2019. *www.pdc.co.il/ind1.htm*.

INDEX

Mounts *(continued)*

    Pluto, 61

  Saturn, 56–57

  Venus, 60

Mystic Cross, 87

O

Owen, Earl, 38

P

Palmar massage, 116

Palmistry

  about, 4–5

  art of, 93

  branches of, 16–21

  laws of, 14–15

  modern, 9–10

  origins of, 6–9

Palmtherapy (Zwang), 10

R

Readings

  comparing palms, 97

  dominant hands, 95–96

  interpretation, 110–112

  nondominant hands, 96–97

  preparing for, 94–95

  querents, 106–108

  sensitivity and sympathy in, 109–110

  steps to conducting, 98–101

  tips for lines, 89

  of your own hands, 108–109

Reflexology, 116

Ring of Apollo, 83

Ring of Saturn, 82–83

Ring of Solomon, 82

Roman Empire, 7

S

Saturn Line. *See* Line of Fate

Scams, 4–5

Self-discovery, 22–23

Simian Line, 7, 14, 70–71

Skin thickness, 41

Spirit (internal power), 15

Splinters, 48

Square fingertips, 86

Star, 85–86

Subconscious mind/energy, 14–15

T

Tao Te Ching, 107

Telepathy, 60–61

Thumbs

  flexibility of, 40–41

  length of, 43

  revelatory power of, 50

Travel lines, 84

"Trigram" patterns, 7

Triradii, 18–19

W

Warner, William John (Cheiro), 9

Warts, 47–48

Whorls, 18–19

Wilcox, Ella Wheeler, 4

Willpower, 15

Z

Zwang, Moshe, 10

ACKNOWLEDGMENTS

I'd like to take this opportunity to thank my wife and daughter for putting up with me and my quirky interests for all these years. I admit that I can be pugnacious and opinionated at times (but only on days ending with a "y"), yet you still support me and haven't kicked me out yet. My love for you knows no bounds.

To Grandmaster James Lacy, I cannot thank you enough for all your instruction and support. You helped me learn how to be ready to raise a child. You are very much missed in this world, yet your presence is still felt.

To John R., I might call you by a name that suggests your mother and father were never married, but you were always there, for decades, supporting me in all my bizarre interests.

And, finally, to my dad. Your loss was my gain. I hope that, at last, I have made you proud.

ABOUT
THE AUTHOR

 **Kenneth Lagerstrom** is a professional cheirologist. He acquired his interest in palmistry from his father, who had lost both hands as a teenager. Kenneth began his research and study of the human hands at age eight to better understand how and why his hands were different from his father's. A wonderful school teacher and the school's librarian helped him on this path of study by giving him full freedom and access to their library, of which he made full use.

Kenneth has spent his life studying everything he can find relating to the hands, from sleight of hand to martial arts. Palmistry became a focal point in his life, and he created www.HumanHand.com. After developing his own unique system of hand analysis, known as Holistic Cheirology, he became a partner in developing the Avdeychik/Lagerstrom system of fingerprint analysis and statistical combinations.

Kenneth achieved the titles of *shi fu* and *lohon* in the 18 Taoist Palms system of Kung Fu (Sup Bat Mo Jung Pai), specializing in hand positions and movements for both meditation and self-defense. He received the 2001 Year of the Volunteers Award from the Government of Canada for contributing his research on identifying genetic defects from fingerprint combinations. He lives on the west coast of British Columbia, Canada, with his wife and daughter.